# ROSARY ROUNDS
A Life Revisited

# ROSARY ROUNDS
A Life Revisited

✢

Joseph Galagan

Copyright © 2014 by Joseph C. Galagan

All rights reserved. No part of this publication may be reproduced, stored in a retrieval system, or transmitted, in any form or by any means, electronic, mechanical, photocopying, recording, or otherwise, without the prior written permission of the author.

Cover Design by Elizabeth J. Toney, B.F.A.

ISBN-13: 978-1502547293
ISBN-10: 1502547295

*Printed in the United States of America*

*To Katherine (beloved spouse and talented editor)*

And family and friends ...

Thanks for the memories.

# CONTENTS

*Introduction*   *viii*
1   The Yellow Lunchbox   *1*
2   Learning to Speak   *5*
3   Changing Seats   *8*
4   A Journey to Nome   *12*
5   Waterfall   *15*
6   The 22nd Street Braves   *17*
7   The Match   *21*
8   Hoop Time   *25*
9   Rosary Rounds   *33*
10   Shamrockville   *40*
11   Checks and Balances   *45*
12   The "D" Class   *49*
13   The Pirate from Rome   *53*
14   Bathing at Lourdes   *57*
15   T-Town Shuffle   *61*
16   The Space Sisters   *67*
17   The History of Jazz   *73*
18   The Green-Eyed Monster   *78*
19   Southern Matters   *83*
20   Irish Chapters   *88*
21   To the Edge of Inishmore   *95*
22   Meeting James Joyce   *102*
23   Crossroads   *108*
24   Upstate   *113*
25   Rehabilitation Road   *118*
26   Departures and Awakenings   *123*
27   A Closing Hymn   *131*

# INTRODUCTION

Memories come in different forms. Some are tied directly to past events, vivid in scope and easily recounted. Others are more vague; dreamlike in their conception, remembrances of things here and there, thoughts and images flashing and then fading into obscurity. But taken all together, memories are what author Nancy Venable Raine has called the "the raw material of our personal narratives, the insubstantial and elusive elements out of which we fashion and refashion our lives into patterns of meaningful sequence".

I came to engage my own memories one morning soon after I retired from a thirty-year career in counseling. I was sitting at a desk in front of my home computer staring at a blank screen, determined to begin a writing project. It was a bright morning in early September, the beginning of a school year, and I was in an upstairs room looking east beyond the Cascade Mountains towards Snoqualmie Valley where I had spent a quarter century occupying a counselor's office in a public high school. During that time, I had written a lot: policy and procedure outlines, informational presentations, and most notably, letters of recommendation, all based on student relationships and interviews. There were many lives and circumstances related to me in my office, hundreds upon thousands before my counseling tenure came to an end - each student with a story or more to tell - each student remarkable in their own way. I described their lives to the best of my abilities, sharing their successes and hardships, hopefully opening doors to further ventures.

Later, when it came time to actually put new thoughts into words, I felt compelled to tell my story. Having related the experiences of so many others for such a long time, it seemed the right thing to do. Instead of speaking about *them*, all those aspiring and blossoming students, I would now speak to my life. Personal history served me well in this context. Starting with my earliest memory, a particular day at age five, I began to piece together a chronological narrative of important life occurrences. Once started in the writing process each memory led to another, a flash flood of remembrance detailing past episodes, conversations and telltale moments. My life unfolded as if shaking out a worn rug, the dust scattering to the wind exposing a smooth and even pattern of growth. It took hold of me, with time moving from the present to the past, my mind calling up images and encounters long dormant or forgotten. When the writing came to a close there were twenty-seven completed chapters, a life revisited, ending at a year in my early thirties when I became a school counselor (a book unto itself and the subject of a future narrative).

*Rosary Rounds* is a testimony to all that we carry within ourselves. We have many lives and histories intricately intertwined to create one defining person. I went in search of this person and found him amidst the landscapes of place and family. He spoke back to me. Here I am, he said, Remember? Just reach out and ask and all will be revealed.

Joseph Galagan<br>
July 24, 2014

And I remember it all. Seems strange for a grown man to keep so many bits and pieces from being small, but it's a house I'm building for myself with a roof of remembering to put over my head. Something to lie under and hear the rain falling on at night. I take what I have and I make what I can with it. Some of it is edge and some is smooth, but I take it all and I use it to make me a place big enough to get inside.
                                                Margaret Wrinkle
                                                      *Wash*


Memory demands so much, it wants every fiber told and retold.
                                                  Denise Levertov
                                 *This Great Unknowing: Last Poems*


What is the self? It is the sum of everything we remember.
                                                Milan Kundera
                               *The Book of Laughter and Forgetting*

# 1

## The Yellow Lunchbox

It is my earliest memory - a yellow lunchbox, open and sitting on the kitchen table, packed with items for the first day of school: a peanut butter and jelly sandwich on white bread, an apple, a hostess Twinkie (a personal favorite) and the requisite white napkin. It was my mother's doing. In one of her moments of Saturday shopping, she must have spotted the lunchbox sitting on the shelf at the Five and Dime on Proctor Street or Rhodes Department Store or maybe the Big Value Grocery up and around the corner from our house on North 22nd Street. Something about the lunchbox spoke to her: the spring-like colors and swirls and intricate patterns of what looked like lace decorations of flowers and leaves. It may have been a woman's intuition, a spark of remembrance from her own childhood in Minnesota, something to do with morning light and graceful gardens. So she reached up and took it into her hands thinking, wouldn't this be a nice lunchbox for young Joey who is soon to begin kindergarten. Wouldn't he look the stylish boy: stripped t-shirt and corduroy pants, wavy hair and a happy-go-lucky smile, tripping along to school with a yellow lunchbox in hand, ready and willing to begin a new experience in life.

But standing there that first school morning and gazing upon the lunchbox, I felt trepidation and fear. This was not the lunchbox for me. These were not the right colors or designs. Having three older brothers, I knew what a real lunchbox should look like. Where were the depictions of Superman or baseball players or dump trucks or red rocket ships? Sure, the lunchbox was square with a snap-shut lid and it was built of the standard tin material that made a thin echoing sound when dinged or knocked. And inside was a small thermos for milk or juice which came with a locking mechanism to hold it in place. It was all as expected, just the kind of lunchbox other boys and girls would have at school. Yet, at that moment my world felt upside down. I was frozen in place, unable to move, overwhelmed by feelings of panic, incapable of imagining ever setting foot on a playground or classroom with that lunchbox in hand.

Close by stood my mother, cheerful and patient, helping my other siblings prepare for the school day. It was a hive of activity with half-dressed children ("Mom, I can't find my shoes"), bowls of cereal, bathroom stops and constant checks of the kitchen clock. I was aware of my surroundings. I knew I was one amongst others, number four of six children, a younger child in a household of numerous family members all with their different needs and desires and personalities. I wanted to cry out, to demand attention, to tell all of the injustice of the yellow lunchbox. Yet it was not to be. Pressing time and kinetic energy rushed us all out the door and into the green two-toned DeSoto parked in front of the house. We piled in, restless, nervous bodies with pencils, paper and lunches in hand, sweaters and windbreakers close by, and headed out, destination: school. And there on my lap, clutched with knuckle-white small fingers, sat the yellow lunchbox.

Lowell School was a short distance from our house, just a mile or so east along the curvy and hilly roadways of Tacoma. From 22nd Street we turned right onto Alder Street, right again on 24th, and then proceeded down past Rosemont Avenue and the Yakima Street Bridge (below which lay a deep and twisting gulch). Along the way, I sighted familiar places: the grassy park strip on Cedar Street where we often played daring games of sport, Tony's Gas Station, the steep and forbidding Carr Hill, and finally the back side of Lowell School with its big glass windows and sloping bank. As we pulled into a side street and parked, I felt lost and defeated; there was no way to avoid what was to come. I would have to face my worst fears. Soon I would be standing in front of my peers, trembling in place, mom by my side, with the yellow lunchbox an unwelcome companion.

Up the sloping side entrance we went, hand in hand, through the doors, down the long hallway, until we came to the kindergarten classroom of Mrs. Larson. Here were other mothers and children, everyone anxious yet excited, all awaiting the first bell. I kept the lunchbox hidden, draping my windbreaker over it as best I could while eyeing my mother as she conversed with the other parents. Then into a cloakroom we all went, finding our names conveniently located next to coat hooks. Nearby were also low level cubbies for books, shoes, blankets, supplies, and lunches. These I eyed with amazement. I quickly placed the lunchbox, along with my other personal items, into one of these cubbies, sight unseen, owner unknown, and wandered out into the classroom. I experienced then a feeling of tremendous relief; no longer holding the lunchbox had made it an object separate from me. It had no bearing on my identity, no pull on my fragile existence, if need be it could now be denied and disowned. It was a moment of exhilaration and one that was to last for the remainder of the school day. At lunch, I slipped my food out of the lunchbox (leaving it and the thermos secretly tucked in the cubby) and walked to the lunchroom smiling and nibbling away at the golden delicious Twinkie.

Later, as school was let out with a flash of running and screaming kids going every which way, I met my older brothers at a corner spot on 21st Street. They would be coming down the hill from the neighboring St. Patrick's Catholic School wearing their green sweaters, white shirts and salt & pepper cords. Together we would begin the walk home, sometimes on the main roads, sometimes through alleys and back streets, sometimes stopping along the way for penny candy at nearby Frederick's Drug Store. This first day of school found us heading back on Yakima Street. I was a little behind, walking slower, dragging my feet, not included in the play and talk of older brothers experiencing the rituals of higher grade levels. By the time we arrived at the Yakima Bridge, I was a full half-block in the rear. Instead of racing ahead to catch up, I stopped and climbed up onto the concrete bridge railing and looked far down at the distant rocks and trees of the gulch. I sensed an opportunity and quickly dropped my yellow lunchbox over the ledge, watching it forever free fall to its untimely demise. It was then that I ran with full speed, whooping and jumping in the air until I reached my unsuspecting brothers. Upon stopping and pondering my impromptu decision, I also knew what I had done was wrong, that there would be a price to pay, and that my mother would be at home waiting for me with open arms and unhappy questions.

When the moment arrived, I looked up into her disapproving face and lied. I told her I had left the yellow lunchbox out on the playground during lunch recess. Somehow it had disappeared. It was nowhere to be found; not returned to the classroom, not in lost and found, not anywhere to be seen. I chattered that maybe someone had walked off with it, taken it home to keep in their room, to use for button collections or doll clothes. Ah, she hesitated, her face suddenly flushed, a dim light of understanding appearing in her eyes. She turned away to go on to the next chore, the next child, the next in an endless series of parenting tasks.

I spent the remainder of the school year carrying my lunches in brown paper bags. No new lunchbox appeared, no further questions or discussions took place. I was left alone with my own mixture of contrary emotions: relief and guilt, pride and anguish, happiness and regret. Nothing hurt more than the lie I had spoken to my mother; she was my greatest fan and I had not been truthful. I was disappointed in myself, in my notable weaknesses and delicate identity. Young though I was, I understood there was much growing up yet to come … much more in the way of becoming a better person and more worthy son.

# 2

## Learning to Speak

Lowell School sat perched on a hillside overlooking Commencement Bay and the old town neighborhoods of Tacoma. From the glassed-in classrooms on the upper floor one could look out over houses and treetops all the way to Vashon Island and distant headlands. To a child the school seemed a world unto itself, for all one needed was right there enclosed within its walls and playgrounds. Here were cheerfully colored hallways, an inviting main office with steep stairs leading down to a side street entrance, lockers and numbered rooms, a cafeteria with a small front stage and tables that could be folded up and stowed away, and outside where live action recesses took place, iron monkey bars, swing sets, tether ball poles and even a covered area for basketball and hopscotch. It was an ideal setting for learning and gathering with new-found friends and teachers.

On certain days of the week, I walked over to the main office and into a private room to meet with a speech teacher. This was usually in the morning, an hour or so after the school day had begun and before the first scheduled recess period. On such mornings, I felt apprehensive and so would make my way down the empty hallways with slow, uneasy steps, looking around, stalling for time, considering a possible escape into a broom closet or bathroom. Yet on each of these days as required, I eventually found myself face to face with this teacher enunciating words, forming sounds, practicing lip movements and doing what needed to be done for what my mother often referred to as " learning to speak".

Spoken language had been an issue in my immediate family for years. I was not the first nor would I be the last to engage in what later became known as Speech Therapy. An older brother and younger sister both struggled with the impositions of stuttering. Complete sentences did not always come easily for them. Words once begun did not always end. At times, conversing with others was a trial, an episode of personal determination and fortitude. In my case, though I too experienced moments of breaking, lost words (yet on a more infrequent scale), I was not able to completely create word sounds, the phonetics of language behind basic speech patterns and spelling skills. When talking, I would utter funny verbiage for words as if speaking with an old and ancient accent. There were a number of occasions when an unknown adult would stare down at me and ask if I was from New York City. "No," I would reply, and they would follow with, "Well you certainly sound like it." Much later in life, I surmised that maybe these speech issues came to us along an ancestry line, a family branch from rural Ireland, possibly County Meath from which the Galagans hailed and where not long ago there was little schooling, the toils of hard farm work and a disappearing Irish language. Might we have been inherent Gaelic speakers struggling with an imposed English language full of difficult inflections and syntaxes?

Because of my speech issues, I became a silent lad of sorts. Aware of my own language imperfections, I vowed to speak less and listen more. I had also come up against a bit of teasing along the way (as did my siblings) and knew the dangers of meanness and subsequent hurt feelings. So I decided to let actions speak louder than words. I strove to be considerate to others, an attentive student, an able playground companion, and a loyal friend. And I also became determined to take my speaking lessons more seriously. I soon recognized that talking in a clearer and more precise manner might lead to easier life challenges. If I could pronounce words correctly then maybe others would respond to me in a nicer manner. If I could be more comfortable when speaking then maybe I might express my thoughts and feelings on a more confident level. Like all people, I too needed to be seen and heard at important moments. I could not be silent at all times. A voice was required but one others could understand and appreciate.

It came to be that I began to look forward to my speech lessons. Down the hall I would still go but now with a spring to my step and a mission to be accomplished. I became firm in my inner resolution to gradually become a better speaker. It would take time as my teacher reminded me, and patience, and practice, yet I felt hopeful and encouraged (traits she so wonderfully exemplified). I likewise had support at home and good modeling as well; my siblings, those with their own speech issues, and another with polio, were persistent and courageous in their daily affairs and forever kind and fun-loving in their life experiences. In a sense, we were in it together; responding to all that life and family had dealt us, striving to make do and come out ahead.

There was a last visit or two to the speech room. The teacher and I would look out the windows together and carefully pronounce the names of things incorporating colors, shapes and objects: "the blue sky, the green trees, the round ball, the silver airplane, the square houses." There was light coming through the glass, bright and radiant, and lightness in my posture and voice. I was entranced and clearly coming through, touching on perfect sounds, speaking to her, hearing my own words, lost in the tones and vivid images of spoken language.

# 3

# Changing Seats

A memorable change occurred at the beginning of third grade. It was like a storm surge washing away all former familiarities and replacing them with new landscapes and characters. No longer in direct need of twice-a-week speech therapy at Lowell Public Elementary, I transferred to St. Patrick's across the street where three older siblings were already in attendance. It was newness personified: a new school year, a new building, a new grade, a new uniform, and a new group of classmates and teachers. I was taking another step, and though excited, there were lingering feelings of anxiety and alarm. I was scared, nervous, and somewhat stunned into silence when the school year began and I found myself sitting in a 3rd grade classroom under the tutelage of Sister Clara.

I quickly noticed that St. Patrick's was a different school environment. Not quite the sometimes noisy and rambunctious setting of Lowell, the students in this Catholic domain sat straight in their chairs and did not interrupt or speak out randomly (I soon learned they were reluctant to do so for fear of possible censure and reprimand). The building also caught my interest with twisting wooden staircases leading from a basement lunch area and interior play space up three flights of floors to a top level. Here one could find the older students, the 7th and 8th graders, some of them tall and of teenage appearance. One did not just randomly walk up to the third floor. It was known to be off limits to the younger grade levels, a remote area requiring a different set of social clues and skills. Being so, it soon became apparent that each student had their specific place in this school. The setting was structured and organized with the focus directed on disciplined learning, personal values and Catholic religious practices. It was also a tightly controlled setting administrated by the ever-omniscient black and white-robed Dominican nuns.

On my first day, I began my classes in a homeroom located on the main floor not far from the office and school entrance on J Street. Everyone was dressed alike with the girls in their plaid skirts, white blouses, green button-up jumpers and more likely than not, saddle shoes. They often wore knee-high socks and in the winter full-length tights in shades of green, black or white. The boys also came prepared with the same blends of green and white only with v-neck sweaters and durable corduroy trousers. It was like a festival of earthy and heavenly colors: green for our garden mascot, the shamrock, the flower from Ireland where St. Patrick had driven the snakes into the sea; and white for the symbolic clouds above, the kingdom of angels, saints, the resurrected Christ and God the Father. It felt comforting to sit in the classroom rows, everyone matching and sequestered in this blessed context.

In the beginning all seemed right and fine. I made a friend named Kevin and even visited his home one Saturday afternoon for lunch. It was in a different neighborhood, one I had never seen before with large mansion-type houses and an enclosed outdoor swimming pool close by. We ate in a warm kitchen at an old table with his other siblings coming and going and his kind mother close by. It was good to be somewhere else: to sit amidst a different family and see how others lived and got along. Kevin was a classmate at St. Patrick's who sat across the aisle from me. He was a jolly fellow with a loud laugh. And he was smart: quick on the mark and dead right on his school work. In due time, I came to envy his casual successes.

As the school year progressed, I began to feel a little uneasy. Something was wrong, out of sync like a clock slowly losing its hold on time. I would look around at the other 3rd grade students so diligent and efficient in their studies and wonder what was holding me back. The academic work seemed difficult and overly taxing. I was confused by many of the assignments and often not able to complete in-class projects within the allotted time. My confidence was wavering and yet I didn't ask for help nor communicate my struggles to others. Caught up in my ever prevalent doubts and disappointments, I hid behind a veil of quietude and shyness.

However, my parents were not fooled. I can picture them speaking privately to each other as they sat at the kitchen table after dinner, sipping their Lipton tea, my mother savoring a cigarette, commenting on the changes they had seen in me during the past months. "What is the matter with Joe? Where is the helpful and smiling child? Where has he gone to? Who is this other fellow, avoiding others, closing himself in his room, not present or noticed?" Their intuitive concerns were probably great enough that action was taken: a conversation or two with me ("What d'ya mean … there's nothing wrong … I'm O.K.") and then soon after a contact with the school and Sister Clara. They had become well acquainted and comfortable with St. Patrick's over the years attending many open houses and pancake breakfasts, driving to and from C.Y.O. sporting events, and establishing themselves as active people in the parish church through reliable appearances at Sunday masses and memberships in such organizations as the Knights of Columbus and the Women's Philomena Society. My mother most likely made the initial phone call.

"Hello Sister Clara. I hope all is well with you. This is Bernice Galagan, Joe's mother."

"Good day to you Mrs. Galagan. It's nice you are calling. In fact I was soon to contact you."

"Is that right Sister? Is it about Joe? His school work?"

'Yes it is Mrs. Galagan. Yes it is."

It was not long after this conversation that I found myself one Monday morning standing outside the 2nd grade classroom of Sister Charles. My mother was present and we were waiting for the first bell to ring. Over the previous weekend mom had told me I was to have a new teacher come Monday. I was being moved back to 2nd grade. Here, she counseled, I could start over and find an easier way through the Catholic school. And since I knew 2nd grade already and was such a bright boy, I could help some of the other students. It would all be for the better.

I knew she was right. Third grade had proven too difficult. Yet, I doubted my ability to help others with math or penmanship or spelling. I was just hoping for a little relief, a moment to find my stride, to somehow catch up and achieve in school on an equal level with others.

As mom and I stood outside this ground floor classroom and watched the 2nd graders line up, I steadied myself for what was soon to come. I would be asked to stand up and be introduced. I might have to say my name and maybe tell others my favorite sport, my favorite food, my favorite pet, or my favorite school subject. It would be an awkward moment. I might feel ashamed, or I might feel alone, or I might stumble over my words. I wasn't yet sure. Just then, Sister Charles came out of the classroom and walked up to us and said good morning and welcome. She knew my name and leaned down and laid her hand on my shoulder. Her smile was a ray of sunshine, her face clean and young and full of delight and care. Once all the other students had entered the room, she guided me through the door saying she had a special seat picked out just for me.

Up the left aisle we went, two desks side by side in each row, until we came to an empty seat. I sat down, lifted the wooden cover and arranged my pencils and paper in the storage space. I hoped to be invisible. I tried to stare straight ahead, to not look at others knowing that everyone might also be looking at me, the new kid. I soon felt a slight poke in my left arm and slowly glanced over to my seatmate. It was someone I recognized, a girl from the playground who often joined in on "red rover" and softball and ran faster and played harder than some boys. I had noticed her before yet never talked to her. She was different in some way, cute and outgoing and brave. Before she said her name, I had a prevailing sense of good fortune. I thought to myself, whoa, how lucky, I get to sit next to her … I guess 2nd grade won't be so bad after all.

She smiled and said her name was Jana.

Yes, I thought. Jana is her name.

"Hi," I replied, "I'm Joe."

She paused and looked at me with a funny grin and twinkle in her eye and said, "I already know that."

*It became a friendship that lasted well into the ages.*

# 4

# A Journey to Nome

Walking into Sister Cecilia's classroom was like taking a step into a foreign culture. On the walls were painted masks, engraved wooden paddles, fur skins and photos of snow-covered dwellings. Along the windows, intermixed on shelves with books and school supplies, were numerous drums and woven decorated baskets, some small in size and others large enough to hold playground equipment. It was a striking cacophony of objects, shapes and colors. The room whirled around and around and sang to me like no other place I had ever encountered.

Sister Cecilia was a young Dominican nun, plump and gregarious with an infectious energy. Up front she would hold court, smiling and laughing and bouncing along while conducting the daily affairs of our third grade education. She caught my attention. I enjoyed her happy and nurturing nature, her ever-present enthusiasm, and her love of music, art and storytelling. I came to see her as a magician wrapped in nun's clothing. She could conjure up images of fantastic places, recite poetry and tell riveting tales, and sing songs of times long ago and almost forgotten. I was captured and held spellbound by her presence and by the room she had created around us.

She came directly to St. Patrick's from Nome, Alaska. There she had spent a number of years teaching in a Catholic mission school for Inupiat Eskimo children. It was a far northern region, above Puget Sound and Canada on the wall map, up distant coastlines to the cold shores of a place she referred to as the Seward Peninsula. In some of her photos, we saw people standing on beaches dressed in fur-lined hooded parkas, boats and fishing gear scattered about, young and old gathered together as if awaiting the arrival of family members still out on seagoing missions. There were also photo images of whales, walruses, slippery-looking seals and deer-like creatures she called caribou. It was a fantastic setting: remote, icy and dangerous. Here were dogsleds and igloos and salmon fish drying on timber racks and being cooked over outdoor fires. I came to see it as a water world. Nome was a place on the edge of the continent, where the Eskimos lived, went to school, and made a life for themselves so different from my own in Tacoma.

With purposeful design, Sister Cecilia immersed this world into our classroom. Before long, we were in tune with the sounds and rhythms of the native people from Nome. All that Sister Cecilia knew of Inupiat culture she shared with us. Between customary lessons of spelling, math and Christendom, she wove in the history, geography and folklore of the Inupiat nation. Out came the drums, the songs, and the spoken stories of survival and hardship. Soon we were weaving baskets and watching Inupiat dance moves and learning about the great whale hunts. Sister Cecilia was a believer, a loyal disciple of the Inupiat ways, herself a bit Eskimo after years of teaching and living there. It was a sight to behold, this round-faced nun at the head of the room becoming one with the natives and relishing in all that Alaska had gifted to her.

I became entranced with the legends of the Inupiat people. The phrase "hunter-gatherers" stuck in my mind. There were also class lessons on the history of the Alaskan Gold Rush involving Tacoma and Seattle. I had seen faded photographs in books of crowded steam ships and bearded gold miners and boardwalks in muddy towns with heavily laden pack-horses standing bent and tired outside old storefronts. It was like being exposed to a new universe: the more I learned the more I wanted to learn, the more I saw the greater the thirst I had for seeing more.

It so happened that each Saturday afternoon brought an opportunity to visit the nearby Proctor neighborhood McCormick Branch of the Tacoma Public Library. We would all walk up together from Alder Street, siblings and friends, through rutted alleys and past familiar basketball hoops, climbing hills until emerging across the way from Washington Elementary. We would then line up and enter the heavy main wooden doors of the McCormick building. When stepping in there would always be a noticeable hush and sense of quiet. I would weave my way to the children's area to look for Alaskan adventure stories and Indian fables. The search would begin and I would eventually leave the library with a book in hand, trooping home with the others, eagerly awaiting the chance to be in my room lost in words and pictures.

At the end of the school year, I said my good-bye to Sister Cecilia and to all the artifacts scattered throughout the classroom. The wall masks were so real and lifelike I had at times wondered if Eskimo ghosts might be present, lurking within that space, infusing us with Inupiat smells and voices. I knew I had taken a journey with Sister Cecilia, not only to Nome but also to someplace within myself, a region of faraway places and remarkable landscapes and hints of greater things yet to learn and experience.

# 5

# Waterfall

A vast world of water lay in front of me, stretching for miles and miles with no land in sight. Out in the distance, waves were rolling shoreward suddenly to emerge as breakers thundering upon the beach on which I stood. On this day the skies were clear, the sun warm and brilliant and the wind quiet and even like the gentle touch of a hand across my face.

On first impact the water was icy cold, numbing my toes almost instantly. Back and forth I went out into the tide, each step a little further, a bit deeper, but each time also running back to the safety of the shore as soon as a wave approached, staying just barely ahead of the onrushing roar. It was a game of tag I was playing with the ocean, running and jumping and chasing the water out on the riptide and turning and fleeing away again to avoid being touched and captured by the returning water.

Feeling braver, I ventured further out with each successive wave action. I could feel the water sucking at my feet as if trying to lure me into her gloomy depths. Once or twice, the water encircled my ankles and came menacingly close to my knees. I began to feel uneasy, isolated, far from the security of bare sand and beach. Just as I turned to head back in, I suddenly found myself engulfed by a surge of wave that had somehow snuck up behind me. I was swallowed up and knocked off my feet. Water was everywhere, rushing by, swirling in all directions. I could sense my hands and feet flailing in the torrents, attempting to grasp hold of something firm and level, a possible hold on life. I then felt the swift undercurrent of receding water straining to pull me further outward, to hold me prisoner, never to relinquish its liquid chains. I began to panic, to struggle, to wrestle mightily with all the elements around me: the water, the sky above, the noise, and my own gasping breath. Fear and dread overtook me. The ocean was in control. All seemed hopeless. I was being taken away, swept to sea, soon to succumb to watery depths. To my surprise I somehow managed to find a foothold. My toes struck ground and the wave lifted me head first out of the water. I found air and saw the dunes and my mother in the distance standing and looking and then running towards me with arms out and her mouth open shouting words. Though still standing, the water was deep and surging and pulling me in circles. I screamed.

"Mommmmmmmm!"

She was coming ever closer, aware and reaching towards me. Her presence gave me strength. I fought harder and with more determination. Each motion was forceful, my small body against the furious ocean. Keeping my balance and never losing sight of her face and her red jacket flapping as she ran, I plunged and crawled and threw my way out of the water onto dry land and into her arms for an embrace forever eternal. And yes afterwards, the tears, sobs and incessant shaking that took hold of me there on the beach, frightened and stunned but safe once again.

And then the terrible nightmares that summer and after.

The remembrance of sheets of water and drowning visions and joyful survival.

And of my young life once forsaken and then restored.

# 6

## The 22nd Street Braves

The north end of the city of Tacoma sits on a series of embankments and bluffs overlooking Commencement Bay. In this part of town, all roads north and west eventually lead down to the water by way of hills, ravines, main roads and parklands. From the flat, plateau-like streets up on top there are numerous descents to Old Town and waterfront environments. Just walk down Alder Street until you come to North 29th and the salt water vistas begin. One sees Vashon Island, Brown's Point, and ever stretching bodies of land surrounded by glistening water. To the distant right, below downtown, sit the industrial tideflats dominated by smokestacks, shipping cranes and long, horizontal buildings housing foundries, wood mills and supply companies. The Puyallup River runs its course south of the city through adjacent valleys until emptying into the bay alongside these buildings, often turning the smoky blue water of Puget Sound muddy brown. In the 1960's era, the St. Regis Paper Company stole the show with its massive buildings, billowing smoke and ever present fragrances. Driving by Tacoma on Interstate 5 often brought out the response, "Ah, the aroma of Tacoma."

If one went straight an additional block past North 29th and took a left on North 30th (traveling the hillsides and eyeballing the coastline below) soon a massive brick tower would appear in the distance. It belonged to what was once the largest copper-smelting enterprise in the world. And it too spewed smoke, a sulfur smelly mixture that would sometimes drift over the north-end neighborhoods causing ghastly short coughs and crude remarks. The waterfront here was a series of ore mounds, railroad tracks and crusted buildings. Arsenic (we eventually learned) was everywhere - in the soil, the air, and the water. Invisibly, it fell to earth and attached itself to whatever it could find including nearby gardens and when wind aided, onto lots and homes of distant headlands. Yet, just beyond this moonscape, on the other side of a blind curve tunnel, one could meander through the broad expanses of the township of Ruston, then down and into a beautiful peninsula of tall trees and long beaches. It was Point Defiance, a timber-laden park within the city, bordering the waters of Commencement Bay and offering stunning views of shorelines and the majestic Narrows' Bridge.

It was within this greater Tacoma region that we staked out our territory. From North 21st to 26th and then from Alder to Oak, we rough-and-tumbled and recruited able bodies to join our cause. It was really no more than an eight-block city radius but there were kids galore and it felt like a kingdom atop a concrete hill fort. Just in our immediate vicinity were vacant lots, hidden alleyways, broad streets, and a nearby small university which happened to provide a swimming pool and a wide open field for sporting contests. It was a piece of paradise and we claimed it as our own.

The idea in those days was to be outside as much as possible. Our parents also believed in this concept, often shooing us out the door saying things like, "Have fun, go play with your friends, find something to do" and away we went scattering in various directions. Of course there were chores to be done on weekend mornings and summer obligations as well, but these were just momentary delays in the greater scheme of things. Most non-school days found us out of the house early and home late, around dusk, coming in just before full darkness descended on the neighborhood.

Left to our own devices, we organized games of chance, established meeting spots, and became explorers of all that North Tacoma provided us. We found places to shoot basketball (the green hoop), play baseball, build camps, go fishing and rendezvous with school friends from other neighborhoods. Rides were not provided nor were parents kept in the know. We just went about the rituals of childhood based on instinct. Run, skip, bike or walk, we were adventuresome and clever and it felt like a time of endless freedom.

Each fall, we got our friends together to form a football squad known as the 22nd Street Braves. There is an existing photo of us standing on a curbside, a ragtag group of boys tall and short, helmets and shoulder pads askew, all wearing dirty long-sleeved homemade jerseys and tennis shoes. Behind the faceguards were tough grimaces and innocent smiles alike. I recognize the players: Tommy, Scotty, Glen, Jimmy, Mike, Pete and others. And there I am, hovering on the side, Joey G., looking somewhat weary yet standing straight and determined. It must have been a picture taken by a parent during one of our practices. We would gather at the corner of 24th and Cedar near a wide grassy parking strip and run through plays and signals. I can just see a dad or mom driving up, hopping out of the car and saying. "Line up boys! This is one for the history books."

Jimmy was our quarterback and leader. He could throw the ball further than anyone we knew and had a knack for keeping everyone in their positions. He would stand a few yards behind the center, leaning on his crutches, giving instructions and awaiting the hike. Though stricken by childhood polio, Jimmy was strong and talented. He was one among us, his own person, steadfast in his efforts, and silently admired by many. He coached us through our assignments and prepared us for the big games ahead. We would huddle up in a circle and Jimmy would call the plays. We ran "alley-oops", the "statue of liberty" and "double reverses" and, when in doubt, a simple but dangerous, "go long Scotty and I'll throw it down field". We were a formidable crew, a bit scraggly no doubt, yet anxious and ready to take on all comers.

On a given autumn Saturday afternoon, we would all walk up to a field at the University of Puget Sound to meet an opponent. A few nearby neighborhoods had teams and we would pair up against each other in a battle of young titans. There would be the sounds of "hike, hike" and then the crush of bodies blocking, running, falling and shouting. It was a sloping field so at times you might be going uphill or down. Depending on the day and weather there would be mud holes or wet slippery grass or cold driving wind or torrential downpours. It didn't matter. We played and survived. At the end of the match we would shake hands and mutter words of "nice game" and drag our way back home down Alder Street, sore and bruised and sometimes bloodied.

Win or lose, there was a feeling of exhilaration on these Saturdays. We had fought a good fight and lived to see another day. In our own time and place, in what was then known as the wide world of sports, we too had experienced the thrill of victory and the agony of defeat.

# 7

## The Match

Daylight was beginning to fall and there was an eerie feeling prevalent in the descending dusk. At this time of year, the air was becoming colder and trees were slowly losing their brightly colored leaves. I was alone. There was no one else around: no moving cars, no wayward dogs, no one coming and going on the sidewalks or yards of nearby houses. All I could hear was the cooing of birds in a tree above me. I looked up; it sounded a bit frightening, mysterious, the calls coming from within the darkness of high branches. I paused and took a deep breath. A slight shiver went through me, a momentary stir, my body briefly shaken from my head down through my toes. It passed. I was once again on stable ground looking straight ahead with a purpose in mind. I took a step onto the stairs in front of me, then another, each step a triumph, all the way to the door. The moment had arrived to summon my courage. I then knocked and waited.

It was collection time, the once monthly ritual of going door to door seeking out all my paper route customers and asking for fees. "Hello," I would say, "I'm here to collect for the Tacoma News Tribune." "Already," might be the response, or "Could you come back tomorrow when I have some cash in the house," or "Just a second and I'll get my checkbook." From large brick apartment buildings, to single houses, to multiplexes and townhomes, I would venture forth with my collection booklet in hand hoping for success, a quick exchange of money for a small square paper receipt. The collection process often took time and patience. It could be agonizing and enlightening and at moments just downright bewildering; a look through a door into the lives and living spaces of other people. Over the years of carrying newspapers, I came to better appreciate the places before me: the smells and sounds and rhythms of humanity. But it took a while; I was young and naive and still discovering my own way.

I heard approaching footsteps from inside the house until a man appeared in the small upper window. He smiled and slowly opened the door. He was wearing a white tee-shirt, smoking a cigarette, and looking amused. I noticed his beard, black and full and a touch unkempt. I also remembered seeing him before, once or twice, getting in and out of his car, carrying a briefcase and wearing a long overcoat.

"What can I do for you?" he said.

"I'm collecting for the newspaper," I whispered.

"You are? You must be the paperboy," he replied.

"Yes I am."

He stood a moment longer and then leaned forward and stared into my eyes.

"Well, do you know what a paperboy's worst enemy is?" he asked.

I was unsure how to answer. Was this a real question, something I should know but didn't? Was he trying to trick or scare me? I was unnerved by his presence, by his way of speaking and looking at me.

I hesitated, not quite sure of myself, and stammered, "I don't know."

He took a last puff off his cigarette and while exhaling turned to his right where I lost partial sight of him for just a second or two. He then reappeared, the smile back on his face, and said, "Fire!"

A match was struck (I heard it strike and pop) and he thrust the flame close to my face. It was yellow and hot and behind it stood the man cast in shadow and gloom. I turned away by instinct and fled down the stairs and around the corner, my heart racing and my legs turning faster than my body could keep up with. Down the hill I went, stumbling and sucking air, to my bicycle and flight and the open roadways. It all happened so quickly, in just a matter of seconds, but the experience has stayed with me, the ancestral remembrance of fire and fear.

✢

There were other memorable events that occurred during my tenure as a newspaper carrier. The daily routine of spending two hours walking neighborhoods, delivering the "Tribune" and observing life brought many lessons to heart. In a sense each day was a different education; one coped with ever-changeable weather patterns (cold freezing winter days when hands and feet throbbed and became numb to hot, sweaty summer days with the black ink of the newspapers smeared on face and hands); with snappy dogs of all shapes and sizes; with odd people encounters in hallways and back entrances and with strange domestic habitats: some clean and neat, and others chaotic and full of trash. There were swimming pools, back alley brambles, broken garage windows, terraced gardens, dank basements, stately mansions, and brick walls running with water. It was an immense world littered with hidden treasures, endless surprises, and people of all ages, shapes and sizes.

One of the places I remember best is the Crescent Apartments. Curved and painted bluish white, the Crescent had four levels including the bottom floor. It took up a half-block from the alley to the corner and then wrapped around another half-block on the adjacent street. Shaped like a crescent moon, this building had numerous outer doorways leading to different sections of the building and the numbered apartments within. It was a maze with skinny interior stairwells, dead-end corridors, and fuzzy well-worn carpets. I came into each section of the building through open entrances (no exterior locks in those days). Up I would climb dropping papers as I went, quietly making my way like a mouse skirting from one floor to the next. Something about the place disturbed me: the muffled laughter behind closed doors, the pungent smells of cooking, the foreign voices and cries of children, and the darkness caught within the passageways and entrances. It seemed a strange world and I was part of its daily interactions, coming and going on the stairs, silent and hidden, yet always feeling edgy and unwelcome. I often thought of the Crescent as a moon shadowy place, haunted in some way, existing on the fringe of normalcy. Once when approaching the building on an early Sunday morning, I tripped and fell, my heavy bag pulling me over onto the ground. There then came a piercing laugh from one of the upper windows, loud and shrill, as if from a witch or evil sorceress lurking above and watching my actions.

From that moment on, each and every time I entered the Crescent over the years, no matter daylight or darkness, dawn or dusk, the same paralyzing words, around and around, back and forth, filtered through my mind ...

*You are now entering the Twilight Zone.*

# 8

## Hoop Time

There is a distinctive, ornate structure sitting on a cliff overlooking Commencement Bay in Tacoma. It is built of yellowish brick and stands tall with shooting spires coming out of arched rooftops. Next to it is an immense horseshoe-shaped earthen bowl overhanging the water, deep and submerged as if about to fall onto the railroad tracks below. When young, I thought it was a place called Disneyland, a magical kingdom where Mickey and his friends hung out. When driving by, I would say, "Look mom, it's Disneyland," and she would reply, "It certainly looks like it." Later, I would come to understand this building was once a world-renowned hotel gone bust and then purchased by the Tacoma Public School District and converted into Stadium High School. For the longest time,

I just wanted to go inside, to explore the hidden rooms and lengthy hallways and lofty towers. I thought there must be secrets dwelling within its walls or domains of mystical powers. In a young boy's imagination, how could there not be?

It turned out my first steps into the building were through a side entrance onto a low-ceiling upper landing and then down a bank of stairways leading to a basement gymnasium. It was ill-lit, steep and forbidding. It was not what I had expected. But then again, I did not walk across the expansive commons out front and into the main curved doors of the school. Instead, I had been dropped off outside by my father somewhere near the bowl and directed into a steel door enclosure. It happened to be the first night of basketball practice, in the first year of organized teams, grade four, and I remember my confidence level bouncing around like a playground red rubber ball.

The gym itself was enclosed by concrete walls and scattered bleachers. At first glance, everything seemed tight and compact. I could hear voices and resounding echoes off in the corners. Out on the hardwood floor stood a number of kids, some standing in place looking uneasy while others were jumping around, everyone waiting for the practice to begin. In the center of the court stood two robust men, coaches with clipboards in hand, Mr. Mitchell and Mr. Ruth according to their nametags. A call to attention went out and we all gathered around in a semi-circle for instructions. Standing there, I noticed I was one of the taller players. No surprise. It was the same at school, heads taller than nearly all the kids in my class except one or two. I was skin and bones, lanky with a mop of hair and cracked bony elbows. Known to some as long tall Joe Mosquito from up on Alder Street, I stood in the back of the circle eyeballing the group for any familiar acquaintances and possible future competition.

Basketball was an important force in my life from the moment I could pick up a ball and wander out the back porch door of my parents' home. If ever I needed an escape from the sometimes crowded atmosphere in our house, I could find it by shooting baskets. With a ball tucked under my arm, I would head outside with time immortal in front of me. Walking and dribbling was a pastime just in itself. The rhythm of the ball striking the ground would create its own dimension. I would move forward, concentrating on each downward push, first right hand then left, my thoughts slowly drifting free of school, friends, siblings and all matters requiring strength of thought. I would soon find the feel of the ball: the texture, the intersecting ribs, the roundness, the way it bounced back into my hand off the cement or dirt-covered ground. Before long, I would be in my own world, striding and then running, making a quick move to the right, then a dash to the left, imagining breaking free and scoring the winning shot in a close game. It was freedom personified.

There was a hoop up the alley just a few houses away at the Hazelton's garage and I would camp there for hours pumping jump shots and practicing lay-ins. If Mrs. Hazelton's Studebaker happened to be parked outside in the driveway, I would scamper one block up the alley to the McDaniel's hoop or the neighboring green house. No one ever came out and said, "Go away kid, you're making too much racket out here." Rain or shine, early morning or evening, alone or with others, there seemed to be an open invite at all three baskets. It was hoop time and there was nothing sweeter than the sound of the ball swishing through the net.

✤

I made the team that first year and spent two seasons playing for the North End Athletic Association (NEAA) under the leadership of coaches Mitchell and Ruth. They were no-nonsense, disciplined men with a good approach to fundamental skills. They took me aside and had me practice keeping my arms up for rebounds, never bringing my hands down after securing the ball. I would practice catching the ball off the backboard with fingers flexed and opened, my body in an upward motion, landing on two feet squared to the hoop. I would then jump back up, arms still held high, and push the ball off the backboard into the hoop. It was a repetitive motion, one of those important under-the-basket skills for a taller player. I became proficient at reading the ball off the basket and making easy put-back shots. I welcomed the rebounding tussles and skirmishes. I knew within myself that this could be my key to success: not open-court fast dribbling, not long jump shots, but controlling the ball in the key, becoming a paint warrior, worming my way to each and every possible rebound.

We would practice at Stadium a couple times a week and play other recreational teams throughout the City of Tacoma, at times traveling to distant gyms for Saturday games. It was fun and captivating. I can still remember one car trip down Proctor Street on the way to challenge a team called Thomas Finer Foods. They were considered a very talented group of players with a good record: a rival team standing in our way to a league championship. I was nervous in the car, anxious and uneasy, experiencing an ever-expanding knot in my stomach often referred to as the "butterflies". It was game day and much was at stake. Walking from the parking lot into the gym seemed to take an eternity. However, once in the door and onto the floor, all thoughts and nerves slipped away. The focus was on basketball: running plays, teamwork, coaching instructions, fair play and hustle. My father was in the stands that day and it was a tight game, evenly contested. We came out on top, a point or two ahead at the end. It was a memorable victory for our team, one to remember, as was the ride home. My father and I concluded the day with a last-minute congratulatory stop at the 6th Avenue Diary Queen for delicious cherry-flavored Dilly Bars.

✤

The next three years found me wearing a green satin uniform for the St. Patrick's Shamrocks. It was middle school, grades 6-8, and time to engage in Catholic Youth Organization (C.Y.O.) leagues. Our twice a week evening practices took place in the Thomas Aquinas High School gym and all games occurred on Sundays after morning masses. There were other competing schools including St. Anne, Visitation, Holy Cross, Sacred Heart, St. Charles, Holy Rosary and St. Leo. It was a competitive mix of up-and-coming Catholic school kids, most of us to meet and converge later in 9th grade under the blue and white banners of Bellarmine Prep.

St. Patrick's was an athletic stronghold in the world of Tacoma C.Y.O. contests. And my class was no exception. With the personalities of talented players like Frankie O, Smitty, Mac and Ronnie B (who transferred to St. Patrick's in 8th grade), we were tough and versatile. We didn't lose any games in 6th and 7th grade and entered our final year at St. Patrick's as the odds-on favorite to win the C.Y.O. city championship for the third consecutive year. Little did we know at the start of the season that our 7th grade team, also rich in depth and abilities, had been promoted to the 8th grade league (they had been devouring teams in their own grade level for two years). Ultimately, we met in the final Sunday game of the season, both undefeated, both unchallenged, both standing tall and firm. The week leading up to the game was a tense affair at school. There were sidelong glances, a bit of posturing, some bumps in the hallways and the ever-building sense of pressure and tension. Come Sunday we were all ready and willing to go, to finally prove our moxie, to walk out of the Bellarmine gym with the championship trophy in hand.

Mac tells the game line as this: the score was 6-6 at the end of the 1st quarter, 12-12 at the half, 18-18 at the end of the 3rd quarter, and 24-22 at the final buzzer. It was a hard fought two-point victory for the 8th graders. We had won and saved face, we had endured the onslaught of their 6'4" center, shifty guards and brawny forwards. It was an occasion to celebrate and we did with youthful bravado and bragging rights. But it didn't last long. The next Sunday both teams journeyed to Seattle to compete in the greater King County C.Y.O. 8th grade championship tournament. We lost in the first game against St. John's in their home gym, falling behind quickly by 6 to 8 points in the 1st quarter, never really able to crawl our way back into the game. We eventually lost by 4 points with our coach encouraging us to the bitter end, shouting instructions, imploring us to "get the ball to Smitty" as the game clock wound down to 0.00. The 7th grade team fared much better; they won the Seattle tournament to much acclaim and newspaper publicity, and then went down to Portland, Oregon and defeated that city's C.Y.O. champ. They were the toast of the town. Yet in our hearts we knew the one game they did lose that year was to us, their older brethren, the class one year ahead, still proud and defiant amidst our own deeply felt disappointments.

✣

High school basketball was a roller coaster ride of twists and turns and up and down moments of success and failure. I was good enough to make the teams, to stay in the program, and to readily progress in my own maturing hoop skills. I was not the best player nor the worst and there were games where I might be in the starting five, games where I would come off the bench, games where I played full minutes, and games where I languished lost and shaken in confidence and desire. My teammates were good people with different character traits. I found them amusing, gifted, kind and agonizing. Coaches were on a similar scale; some of them I greatly admired and others I found lacking in substance and consistency. It was like weathering different temperatures: hot and cold, calm and stormy, sunshine and gloomy clouds. Each practice, each game brought different challenges and intrigues. I was also changing with new interests and friendships, and more active relationships with the opposite sex. More than anything else, it was a time of growth and inward searching.

During my junior year, I experienced the ultimate extremes of athletic endeavor. The first game of that season found me playing in a swing role: two quarters of JV and two quarters of varsity. I was in the zone that Friday night against Clover Park High School. I couldn't miss; from jumpers to rebound put-backs to fingertip rolls to cross-key slashing drives, all the shots fell in and the numbers piled up. By the end of the four quarters, I had scored 28 points, surprising not only my coaches and teammates but also myself. It was the best performance of my basketball career. It seemed I had tapped a deep well of insatiable energy within myself, an unvanquished source of desire and motivation that carried me to new physical levels. I was soaring, gliding, jumping, and sprinting like I had never done before. It was as if I was playing like my life depended on it. Maybe I had something to prove, maybe it was my time to make a statement, and maybe all the preparation and practices were finally paying off.

The following Sunday morning, I came down to breakfast feeling fatigued and nursing a bad headache. I hadn't been sitting at the table for more than a few minutes, munching on a bowl of cereal, when my mother sitting across from me spoke up.

"There is something wrong with you."

Call it a mother's intuition, a penetrating look into my eyes, a glimpse into my heart and soul, but she sensed that I was not feeling okay. Something was off, and both she and I could feel it. Over the next few days, she took me to see our family doctor and then a medical specialist. Examinations were performed, lab tests were run, and she kept a close eye on my every move. I went to school after each of these morning appointments and then to basketball practice. On Monday, I was put in the varsity starting five: a recognition of my first game hustle and gamesmanship. It was a shining moment; I felt proud and dignified. My teammates were also supportive knowing I had earned the spot, Frankie O and Smitty among them. That made the moment even better, confirmed by their nods of affirmation and smiles of acknowledgement. For the moment, everything was right and good out on the hardwood floor.

However, the flame was burning low. Whatever energy I had once found was soon lost. During practices and the next game early that week, I was lethargic and uninspired. The magic was gone and in its place a tired and forlorn person. Then the diagnosis arrived: Leukemia, and the end of my playing season. It was a moment of compound disappointments, of frightening and confusing news, and of looks of heartbreak in the faces of family and friends. In a few days time, I had traveled from the top of the mountain to the valley floor below. Stunned, I had serious daily misgivings about life and death and the journey ahead.

Over time (including some long days and troublesome nights) and with the love of family and the care of talented medical personnel, I began to slowly find a path back to health and normalcy. There were doses of chemotherapy, radiation treatments and frequent trips to Children's Hospital in Seattle. Once a budding athlete (with my short-lived flare of fame), I was now engaged in a different battle. I sat out that junior year basketball schedule, sometimes sitting in on practices, sometimes attending games, and sometimes avoiding the whole scene. It was hard to watch and not be included. I was on the outside looking in, a different person now, a cancer patient striving to recover and forge a future identity.

The breakthrough eventually happened. One weekend morning I picked up a basketball off the back porch, tucked it under my arm, and headed out to the alley. The Hazeltons' hoop was still there waiting as it always had been. And so were the others. Nothing had really changed. It was still just me and the ball and these once familiar basketball arenas. It was like rediscovering old friendships: someone or someplace you once greatly valued and from which you then moved away. Hello there, I thought, I'm back. I took a few tentative shots, dibbled around in circles a time or two, and then put in a right-handed lay-in. I could sense my strength reluctantly returning, the old magic stirring deep within. It was gratifying. I felt hopeful. I thought, might this moment be the beginning of a comeback? Could I once again find my way onto the court, running and rebounding and sharing time with teammates and coaches? I decided that it was.

So I started over. I kept going out into the alley, alone and determined to make headway. The love of basketball was still there, the moves and turns and dance of hoop. It had not gone anywhere. It had just been denied full existence by unforeseen circumstances. Alley ball was therapy of its own making and one I badly needed. It helped me forget the disease and what might happen, what could happen, and what I didn't want to see happen. It provided a space to once again find the feel of the ball, the rhythm and groove, the energy and flow, and the regained belief in

31

myself as an athlete. All I needed was time.

Many months later on the first day of practice, senior year, November 1972, I was standing with my teammates in the Bellarmine gym listening to coaching introductions. I was still in the midst of chemotherapy but feeling fine. It was a blessing and an emotional moment. I looked around and felt I belonged. I didn't ask for any special favors or hand-holding or unnecessary considerations. I thought to myself while once again enclosed within the walls of basketball fame ...

Just roll the ball out and let's play ... bring it on ... let hoop be the beginning and the end and all things in-between.

# 9

## Rosary Rounds

We all gathered together every Sunday evening. A shout would go out, first up the stairway, then down into the basement.

"It's time for the Rosary."

There would be a shuffling and tramping of feet as children, young and older, made their way from bedrooms and play areas into the living room. Here we would kneel down together as a group, all eight of us, back to back, each person facing a chair, sofa or piano bench, hands folded with black rosary beads entwined to begin the recitations and prayers:

"I believe in God the Father, Creator of heaven and earth ..."
"Our Father Who art in heaven, Hallowed be Thy name ..."
"Hail Mary, full of grace ..."

Around and around we would go, calling forth the mysteries of the rosary: the five decades of repeated prayers, intoning the life of Christ, counting and slowly moving our hands from one bead to the next. First would come the Apostle's Creed and then the Our Father and soon ten Hail Mary's one right after the other, our knees creaking and our backs aching yet each prayer articulated in the cycle until the very end. We would acknowledge the holiness of the Church, seek the blessings of God upon us, and with the lights turned down low, whisper our humble and appreciative thankfulness. Saying the Rosary was a quiet interlude in our home, sanctified and timeless, a brief but important gathering of familiar family souls.

✣

My parents were born, raised and educated as Catholics: my father Cyril James from Irish/German farming ancestors in southwest Minnesota and my mother Bernice Mary Cunningham of Scotch/Irish heritage and a native of Minneapolis. Her father was a train engineer. In one particular photograph he appears short in stature, standing on the platform of a station, a Milwaukee Road baggage car in the background, cap tight and straight and thumb hitched in his belt buckle, surrounded by Bernice and friends and smiling at the camera. I believe he was a quiet man, dignified and loyal and good to his wife and two daughters. I never heard a bad word spoken about Jim Cunningham. He kept to his own business and worked hard as was expected of him. He was dependable and honest, someone you could trust at the helm of a powerful freight train. He spent forty-seven years working for the Milwaukee Railroad and upon retirement was presented with a train lantern, the kind the conductor would swing from the steps of a passenger car signaling "all clear".

Jim's wife was Mary Anastasia Gavin, a stout woman of strong character. To those closest to her, she was known as Maime. Upon marriage, her role in life became that of homemaker and mother. In Minneapolis the family first settled on South 24th Avenue where the two girls, Margaret and Bernice, were raised. Margaret was the first born in 1915: a gentle, quiet, bobbed-hair child who would later during adolescence develop challenging learning and mental health issues. Bernice followed a few years after in 1918. She was a loving younger sister destined for greater achievements. Many of the surviving photographs show a strong kinship between Maime and Margaret. They are often seen near each other, side by side in close proximity, the pair of them bonded together: Maime with her hand on Margaret's shoulder, Maime sitting with Margaret in a group picture, Maime walking with Margaret in the garden behind the house. It is obvious Maime was Margaret's devoted caretaker. She provided home assistance for Margaret for many years until age got the better of both her and Jim. Margaret was then placed in a state institution for adults with special needs. I visited her there once with my mother Bernice. We had come out from Seattle to see relatives. It was somewhere near Rochester, Minnesota and we spent the afternoon with Margaret having lunch and walking the surrounding grounds. I remember the fondness between them; they held hands and walked arm in arm. They were sisters, and though separated by region and age, and maybe also by some distance involving mental capabilities, there were expressions of love, remembrance and acceptance between them. On that day they seemed to renew an important emotional connection; they were two siblings from one family, one cherished home, the children of Jim and Mary Cunningham, patient and loving parents, practitioners of the Christian values of faith, hope and charity.

Bernice attended schools in Minneapolis and was a stellar student. She had an intelligent bright smile, dark curly hair, wore stylish clothes and with her rounded face and button nose was a bit of a head turner. In her 1933 ninth grade yearbook from St. Margaret's Academy, classmates describe her as a "sweet friend", "successful scholar", and a "fine actress". Bernice loved school, embraced learning, and became an avid reader and life-long proponent of education. She excelled in classical studies at St. Margaret's (and later at South High School) yet also took courses in Business and Office Practices which included vocational training in Stenography, Typewriting, and Bookkeeping. These skills served her well in life providing entryway into numerous professional jobs including her first at the Federal Reserve in Minneapolis upon graduation from high school.

In 1942, Bernice made a momentous decision to leave Minneapolis. It was to be her first step away from home, a signature separation from her parents and Margaret. One morning, she and two friends (the sisters Doreen and Mary Healy) boarded a train that was to take them across country to the shores of Puget Sound and Seattle. Along the way they stopped at National Parks where they camped, rode horses and enjoyed the great scenic beauty of the American West. There is a last-minute

35

photo of the ladies boarding the train in Minneapolis, standing on the carriage steps, holding the rails, dressed in fine suit jackets, skirts and hats, and all adorned with flower corsages. There was a large group of well-wishers present to see them off. It must have been a bittersweet moment for many, a good-bye ceremony of sorts. Behind the smiles and Sunday best clothes, I sense a closing of time and the beginning of unexplored chapters.

Upon arriving in Seattle, Bernice settled on Queen Anne Hill in an apartment with the Healy sisters. It was the start of a new experience amidst the shadows of World War II. Times were changing; all things seemed a bit unsettled and tilted. There were formidable foes across the distant seas in both Germany and Japan. A call to action had gone out and many young men had responded. It was also some time during this year, possibly just before she left for Seattle that my father, Cyril James, walked on stage. Bernice had gone to a dance hall in Minneapolis one weekend night with old friends for an evening of table drinks and reminiscing. Within the boisterous crowd were many soldiers and sailors, some on leave and others waiting for their deployment orders. It was an event heightened by the news unfolding in Europe and Asia. Anticipation was in the air, excitement and nervousness in the voices of the U.S. servicemen, and most likely the desire to meet and hold someone close and precious (and in doing so to somehow forget what might lay ahead). Cyril was present, a Navy man dressed in sailor whites. At some point his eyes met Bernice's, an invitation to dance was made and accepted, and a jolt of electricity was felt. It was an evening they both remembered fondly (it likewise happened to be the beginning of a relationship and marriage that was to last for almost forty years).

Cyril hailed from a farming family near the tiny township of Lismore in the far SW corner of Minnesota. The next closest town of any size was Worthington and then further west, Sioux Falls in South Dakota. From Lismore if one looked in any one direction, east, west, north or south, all that came into view were corn and soy bean fields and tall grain silos interspersed between farm buildings surrounded by scraggly elm and ash trees. It was heartland farming and dairy cow country populated mostly by Irish and German immigrants who had worked their way, generation by generation, into the Midwest from the eastern American seaboard. It was a region of struggling farm families, of uncompromising winter weather, of small quaint towns, and of Catholic and Lutheran churches. Cyril was one of eight children born to Robert Galagan and Julia Daldrup. First came two girls, Lola and Vernes, then a boy named Robert who died in infancy (a kernel of corn had lodged and grown in his throat eventually closing off his wind pipe), then another girl, Inez, and finally four boys in succession: Bill, Cyril, Carl and James. Their father Robert was known as a well-intentioned man who chewed a fair amount of tobacco. He was not a particularly good farm manager and over the years often found himself indebted to banking interests. Farming in those times was a difficult way to make a living no matter the determined efforts involved. There was also a big family to take care of. In the end, Robert lost the farm and moved into Worthington with Julia to live out their remaining years. It must have been a sad ending to a long tenure of farming toil and endurance.

I recall a family story of Robert and Julia leaving the farm on the last day by car (chauffeured by Inez and husband Pete) with young James still standing in the farm lot seemingly alone and abandoned. He was the last child at home, sometimes referred to as a rascal of a boy who once brought a dead skunk to school in a paper bag. James was fourteen at the time of his parent's departure (known to all by his middle name Bob) and fiercely independent. He was somewhat living his own life, coming and going and not always around to be considered. He also might have refused to move into town or his parents may have felt that they had lost control of him by then. It is not clear what exactly took place nor was it often spoken about. Young Bob did survive (sleeping in hay barns and working for nearby farming families) and a few years later, at the age of seventeen, he slipped his way into the U.S. Army. He returned and settled in Worthington after World War II with two Purple Hearts in hand, a veteran and survivor of the Normandy D-Day beach assaults.

Mother Julia was a spirited woman who knew her way around animals and was a bit of a trickster. She kept the family afloat, orchestrating farm and household duties and keeping track of the children during their formative years, often driving them in horse and buggy to and from school. She was known as a fun-loving mother with a keen sense of humor and much of her playfulness got passed along to her children. In childhood and adult life they often laughed long and hard, and at any Galagan family gathering there was always a hint of mischief in the air. The men in particular could be boisterous and sarcastic, taking the lead in telling stories and issuing witty anecdotes. And yet there was always the

Catholic doctrine close by. On the farm the family would meet around the pot-bellied stove in the kitchen to say the beloved Rosary - children assembled and accounted for, father Robert lying down nearby recovering from a full day of labor in the fields. There was even the time when Bill took charge of the buggy on the way to school, the horses charging full ahead at reckless speed and the girls in the back all with rosaries in hand praying for salvation. Bill later became known for riding his horse into local bars and raising corn-fed bison. He was Buffalo Bill Galagan, WWII Army Airborne, also a D-Day survivor, one of the next in line of early rising, gregarious, and enduring Galagan folk. The family motto would remain embedded through time: "Work Hard, Play Hard".

This is the world Cyril reluctantly came from. He loved his family and remained loyal to them throughout the years yet he did not enjoy the farming life or the mixed-grade small country day school in the Lismore vicinity. He wanted more and was given permission by his parents to attend high school in Lismore at St. Anthony's Catholic Parish. At that point in history only the girls enrolled in high school. They would work and room full-time in Lismore with local families. Boys of teenage years stayed on the farms, learning agricultural trades and lending helpful hands to the numerous daily farming responsibilities. Cyril was different: he had a sharp mind for numbers and was not mechanically oriented. So each school day morning he walked the long miles into Worthington, participated in his classes, and then walked back home where he was greeted with chores, dinner, and evening homework assignments. He also played basketball at St. Anthony's, tall and lean and listed as a center in the starting varsity line-up.

Like his three brothers, Cyril joined the U.S. Military at the beginning of World War II and was posted to a joint Air Force/Naval 14th Unit base in Kunming, China. This was after he graduated from St. Anthony's, possibly the first Galagan male ever to earn a secondary school diploma. He was assigned a desk job in China, performing the duties of a clerk with the official status of "Yeoman First Class". It must have been the scores on his Navy entrance aptitude test, probably off the scale on adding, subtracting, multiplying and long division. Little did they know then that Cyril would go on in future years to a university degree in Accounting and great success as a public C.P.A.. However, before any of that happened, he was young, full of vigor and living in China. Each day must have seemed unimaginable: here he was working in a military office, far from home, traveling in Chinese rural areas, making friends, playing cards, and coming of age. It was the beginning of his independent life, his first step (and a big one) out of Minnesota and away from the landscapes of cornfields and cow barns.

It was during this time that Cyril met Bernice at the dance hall in Minneapolis. It was before he was posted to China, sometime in 1942. They kept in touch, wrote letters, sent postcards, and visited when he was granted leave to come stateside. It eventually led to a promising relationship and then a marriage ceremony in Minneapolis at Holy Rosary Church on May 4th, 1946. They had found and bonded with each other amidst the distance of war, relocations and uncertainty. Both families were in attendance, the Cunninghams and the Galagans, dressed to the hilt and ready to celebrate, all except Carl Galagan, missing at sea and presumed dead, a Navy casualty, November 1943.

Cyril and Bernice would settle in the Puget Sound region, first Seattle, then Enumclaw and finally on North 22nd Street in Tacoma. Six children were born between 1947 and 1959, four boys followed by two girls. As parents they were caring, resilient, disciplined and honest. They believed in each other and in their children. Education was a priority and Catholic schools and parishes a center point. Like most families, things were not always easy: there were many children, life and health issues, early challenges of a premature first child, then soon a child with polio, and later all the years of teenage growth and development. However, they stayed the course and never wavered in their support and love. They were exceptional people, a devoted couple, two individuals, Cyril James Galagan and Bernice Mary Cunningham, that I am so proud to call my parents.

Their children prospered; all six graduated from college and a number of them earned advanced degrees in fields such as law, public health, counseling, and medicine. With a sense of fortitude passed along through the ancestral lines, these children became a very capable group, manifesting many talents and skills and always a good sense of humor and adventure. They themselves brought ten more children into the world, another generation of like-minded souls, instinctively carrying forth the Galagan and Cunningham dynamics within varied family bloodlines.

And just recently the first of the next generation has arrived.

Welcome Reiss Katherine Galagan - born May 8, 2012.

# 10

## Shamrockville

Things started to look a little more distinctive in 7th grade. The faces of my fellow students suddenly came into clearer focus: their colored eyes and whitish teeth and contrasting smiles. Though we were all attempting to look somewhat alike (with popular clothes' fashions and haircuts), I began to perceive we were really very different from each other. There were short students with awkward gaits, and taller students with floppy shoes, and quiet withdrawn bookish students who preferred to be left alone, and sneaky argumentative trouble-making students often being called down to the main office. Some students began to appear at school with blemishes on their faces and others with greasy uncombed hair and still others with sleepy looks in their eyes and their green sweaters turned inside out. However, the most noticeable were the girls. Something had changed with them and it took a while to figure it out. At first I was in a bit of a quandary. They seemed somehow much older, walking here and there in their tight friendship groups, laughing and sharing secrets and keeping to themselves. Their faces also had a new peculiar shine, a glow of sorts with rosy tones and eye highlights. I felt at a loss. What was happening here? What power and mystery did they share that the boys in my grade did not? I needed to know and began to search for answers.

I first thought back on all my encounters with girls growing up and remembered a few important moments. There was an interaction in 4th grade out on the playground when I mistakenly said the wrong thing to a classmate and she kicked me full force in the right shin. She was wearing saddle shoes and I never saw it coming. The pain was so great I limped into the basement cafeteria holding back tears and hid in a corner. I was probably trying to be funny, hoping to get her attention in the wrong way and paid the price. There was another episode when I told a girl she had "silly germs". This was just after she had been in the front of the class giving a brief presentation and was returning down the aisle to her seat. My comment hurt her feelings and I could hear her behind me sniffling and upset. She didn't look at or talk to me for weeks even though I thought we were friends. And then there was the time when a classmate sitting directly in front of me was lost head down in a book hidden on her lap. The whole time the teacher was talking this student was engaged in silent reading. I thought it was brave of her to sit there not paying attention, not completing her math worksheet, seemingly oblivious to the whole world around her. So I tapped her on the shoulder and whispered, "What are you doing, Sara?" She turned slightly sideways in her desk, lifted up the book and said, "I'm reading *Lord of the Rings*. Don't you know, Joe? It's the best story ever." I felt dumbfounded. Had I miss something along the way? I likewise enjoyed reading but had never heard of the book. Many years later in a future time and age I would come to better appreciate the fascination of Tolkien. At that moment, I was simply light years behind Sara.

In the course of my investigations, I decided to carry on with a few of my own careful devices. It was equivalent to slowly dipping a toe into water to test the temperature. I was tentative and hesitant yet curious. I wanted to better understand the girls in my class. I desired to talk with them privately, to walk down the halls together from class to class probing and seeking out responses. But I didn't want to offend anyone, to cross the line of no-return. I had learned my lessons earlier. It was safer to be on one's best behavior.

So I became more of a smiley, friendly kind of boy. Up and down the school staircases I would go chatting and making eye contact and asking girls about their pee-chee drawings and book covers and homework assignments. If possible, I would try after school to catch up with one or two and tag along for the walk home up and down the hilly expanses of Yakima Street. My efforts were reciprocated. The axiom "ask and you shall receive" rang true. Most of my positive outreaches elicited a similar reaction. Some of the girls were like-minded; they too wanted a more personal relationship, something greater than the usual "go away, leave me alone" statements of past times. This brought about longer conversations on street corners and more penetrating looks when passing in the school hallways. Before long, we were hanging out together, small groups of us, boys and girls, old and new friends and then kind of matching up, not like going steady or anything, but saying we were "with" one another: Joe and Molly, Kathy and Dennis, Kenny and Jana. There was a little hand holding and even a prolonged kiss or two standing in the darkened shade of trees. It was exciting and bewildering. All of us were treading in strange, previously unexplored waters not knowing how deep we might venture.

✢

Eighth grade brought even greater delights. We would now be schooled on the top third floor of St. Patrick's. No longer the younger, unnoticed, lower social stratum in the building, we had finally arrived as top dogs, the then reigning princes and princesses of shamrock school society. Once again, we had taken another step into maturity. Not only did we look a little older but we also felt a little older, more daring, and ready for new adventures. There were skating parties and ski bus trips and visits to see girls during their weekend evening babysitting hours and a memorable Saturday afternoon spin-the-bottle group affair down in old Tacoma at a modern house tucked under blanketing trees. I remember the day well having never kissed so many girls in one wondrous setting. And my two friends felt the same way as we walked home up Carr Hill in mild disbelief, smiling and kidding each other and hoping for a soon-to-be next go-round of face to face encounters.

It was also right around this time of heightened sensory awareness that I suddenly became tuned in to the sounds of music around me. It is true that music had always been there playing on A.M. radio stations like KJR and then on 45 and 33-rpm record players. It could be heard in cars and out front doors and sometimes in the closed rooms of older brothers. But it often felt like background noise to the movie of life being acted out in front of me. I sensed the music but I didn't really listen to it. It was just there filling space as I wandered by thinking my own thoughts. But this changed in due course. One night during this 1968-69 eighth grade year, I was in a basement room with friends when someone put on the first Doors album. Up floated the driving rhythms of "Break on Through" and "Soul Kitchen". I was mesmerized, caught within the dark-voiced, piercing lyrics of Jim Morrison. It seemed the music was entering my mind and body without interference. I was captured by its guitar and organ beats and blend of coursing vibrations. There were songs about back doors and crystal ships and learning to forget and setting the night on fire. I found it powerful and intoxicating. Soon after, on a winter night of cold air and swirling snow, I happened to find myself with a female companion entering the mud porch of her parents' house. Inside a party was in motion, orchestrated by her older brother with friends from Stadium High School. As we stood there in the kitchen, feeling a bit innocent and incognito, I gathered in the music being played out in the front room. It was coming in loud but still seemed far away. Wow, what is that, I thought to myself. I edged closer along the wall, hoping to get a clearer listening place and then it hit me. Bam! It was a roar of guitars and voices cutting the air and looping up, up and tumbling away into rock ecstasy. "Led Zeppelin," someone shouted. Even the name seemed extraordinary.

From there the flood gates opened. Everywhere I turned there was a pulsating musical vein. Right smack in the middle of my parents' living room, shag rug and green and gold sofas galore, sang and danced curly-haired Scotty from across the alley. Our lifelong friend had found the British band "The Animals" much to his liking. He was the neighborhood Eric Burdon, born and raised on the corner of North 24th Street in Tacoma, pumping and swooning with the electric blues music coming out of our Magnavox console. It was also not uncommon for friends to drop by after school with albums in hand. Our house became a listening post; we had the equipment and some spare freedom to entertain others. The space would fill up with musical selections from Van Morrison, The Yardbirds, Jimi Hendrix and others. For many of us, it was the beginning of a lifelong obsession with music in all its forms.

Eighth grade ended with a dance party held outside on a tennis court following our shamrock graduation ceremony. It was a warm night in June with light still visible in the sky and Commencement Bay below us turning a silvery green hue. I remember it as a bittersweet event, a closure and an opening all at the same remarkable moment. You could sense the shyness in the class, no one really wanting to step out front to lead the first dance. We were temporarily lost in our own transitions, looking ahead, knowing change was coming, but not quite ready to move forward. Then it happened. A Paul McCartney song came up on the turntable, a pop-ish tune with flashy rhythms and off we went, pairing up, laughing, acting cool and dancing off all of the pent-up energy held in check by recent formal school ceremonies. The evening turned out to be a blast, a final soaring send-off into a new and immediate future awaiting our arrival.

# 11

## Checks and Balances

The summer before high school was a time of thoughtful summary. It was 1969 and I had reached the reflective age of fifteen in late July. I spent a fair amount of time that summer sitting on the front steps of my parents' house adding things up, attempting to achieve a clearer understanding of self and others. It had been a tumultuous decade, the 1960's, full of mind-boggling assassinations, first President Kennedy in 1963 and then in rapid succession, Robert Kennedy and Martin Luther King in 1968. The Vietnam War was ablaze, a firestorm of images and destruction portrayed nightly on TV news' programs. Many of us knew older brothers involved in the conflict, young men carrying guns and grenades, trekking through jungle landscapes far from the grass-lined sidewalks and square blocks of Tacoma. There were also Civil Rights and Anti-War movements: Dr. King shouting words of reconciliation alongside freedom marches and campus demonstrations which sometimes ended in vivid violence and death. The decade seemed adrift, caught up in turmoil and chaos. And yet out of the gloom there arose repeated messages and symbols of hope, love, brotherhood and harmony. There were music festivals, long-haired hippie folk, peace sit-ins, ascending gospel songs, and endless calls for the government to make things right. It was as if the people themselves were calling things to order, providing a counterbalance to help bring us back to some semblance of justice and fairness before the country completely fell asunder. All this and more defined my early years; it was part and parcel of being born in 1954 and coming of age in the 1960's. I was fifteen, there were August blue skies, and I was eagerly awaiting a different school, a higher grade, and a new opportunity to define who I was.

I happened to live in a household where the sequence and schedule of things were an ongoing important attribute. My father, a businessman and private C.P.A., expected results and that is exactly what he received. The country may have been going to hell in a hand basket during the 1960's but our home life remained steady and productive. We became creatures of habit. Each school morning my father would yell up the stairs, "Time to get up ... up and at 'em." We would rise with sleepy eyes and deep-throated yawns, pulling on our school clothes and stumbling down the steep stairway to get in line for the one household bathroom. Then into the kitchen for bowls of cereal and peanut butter toast and out the door with books and lunches in hand for the mile long walk to St. Patrick's. By the time I was in eighth grade my two oldest brothers were off engaged in university studies and James, closest to me in age, was a junior in high school. It was a family of good students with college aspirations. My father would not have had it any other way.

I remember one night in particular during those years when my younger sister Mary and I were helping Dad with some bookkeeping chores. In the background, the radio was dialed in to a national news broadcast. I could hear what seemed to be distant voices and a tense live coverage of events. We sat on the floor next to the dining room table where Dad was writing away on green accounting tablet paper. Mary was going through boxes and stacking up checks (the kind you wrote when paying bills) and I was putting each pile in numerical order. It was a simple exercise but a time-saving one. Once all the related checks were compiled, we would hand them over to Dad and he would commence with his faster than lightning ten-key machine magic, adding each sum from each check, turning them over, punching the numbers into the ten-key and eventually coming forth with a grand total. Depending on the outcome, a smile or frown would cross his face. He often would recount the figures to make sure all was correct. He took his work seriously and was known for reliability and consistency.

On this night, he suddenly got up from the table and walked across the living room to the console radio. He stood there for a moment intently listening to the news program, eyes down and creases crossing his forehead. He seemed disturbed, placing his hand on the small shelf above the fireplace and then leaning against the wall. I was watching his every move, knowing something was wrong, that something bad had happened in the world, a broadcast of disagreeable events. For a moment he remained motionless, then he turned to look across the room at Mary and me looking back at him. Our eyes met, we were frozen in place awaiting his next gesture, maybe a word or two, or a reassuring grin, anything to help us understand the moment and his discomfort. He turned back to the console and reached in to lower the volume, a slight adjustment on the dial and another to find a different station, a sports channel, probably a University of Washington basketball game. On his way back to the table, he gave us a nod and a silent motion. Keep working, he seemed to be saying, carry on, all will be well and good in due time, just stay to the task and finish the project.

It was later in life, at a more mature age, when I came to fully realize the importance of that evening. Like many men in his generation, my father carried an internal strength. It was not about gushing words and emotional displays, nor the idea of putting on a quick two-step to make everyone feel better or even pretending in some mistaken fashion that all was right in a time of wrong. Instead, it was quiet perseverance and an unquestioning belief that hard times were eventually followed by good times. My father had learned this in his own life through the tribulations of farm poverty, WWII, educational advancement, childhood illnesses, and the ebb and flow of successful business practices. He had worked hard and come a long way to get to that moment in history, his children at his feet, his C.P.A. firm in full swing, and his first purchased house on North 22nd Street. No matter the worldly conflicts, he was determined to hold the line, to give his children a home, stability, and a fighting chance to succeed in life.

I still hold my father within me. At times, looking in the mirror, I

47

see images of him staring back: the bald crown, the wide-set eyes, and the telltale firmness of purpose. I also carry an affinity for the culture and music of the 1960's. I believe in the causes of those times: freedom, equality, social justice, civil rights, and a great society without war and destruction. When I see former military personnel wearing their Vietnam Veteran caps, I feel the urge to stand silent in respect and humbleness, knowing that they fought a difficult battle and survived to live another day. And yet ghosts may remain for many of them, the lingering images of Agent Orange, napalm, and dead and dying comrades and friends.

Maybe Jimi Hendrix expressed it best. He was touched by racism, family strife, drug use and juiced up rhythm & blues music. The era of the sixties covered much of his twenties, the time of nearly all his artistic output. That same August of 1969 he appeared at Woodstock, the now famous joyous celebration of the sixties-counterculture (three days of peace and music). Jimi took the stage with the Band of Gypsies and during his set laid down an electric guitar rendition of the American anthem, "The Star-Spangled Banner". It was a surreal moment, the music beautiful and searing, Jimi the black voodoo child of love playing for the immense white hippie crowd. Mostly it was a song of unity and inspiration and a lasting testimony to an enduring faith in America and democratic ideals. And it came right at the apex of the Vietnam War and civil rights' unrest.

Soon after, near the end of his life in 1970, Jimi Hendrix left us with the following words:

*The story*
*of life is quicker*
*than the wink of an eye*
*The story of love*
*is hello and goodbye*
*Until we meet again*

# 12

## The "D" Class

My high school education began in a classroom filled with comic geniuses. Up and down the rows of desks sat clowns, jesters and mimics all disguised in button-down dress shirts and pressed slacks. Who could have guessed on that first day of school that I was in for some memorable life lessons?

I had landed in what was known as the "D" class via an entrance exam score. Though a fairly good student, I was not an able test taker, often scoring well below the average norms on most large-scale subject evaluations. Coming out of eighth grade and entering ninth thus found me feeling a little embarrassed. In the four levels of academic competency at Bellarmine, a highly regarded college preparatory institution perched on a hillside in Tacoma, I would be starting at the bottom. There would be the brilliant students in the "A" class, the smart achieving students in the

"B" class, the steady non-failing students in the "C" class, and then the "D" class students, the lower one-fourth all heaped together sharing an existence and homeroom down at the end of Freshman Hall.

Bellarmine was in itself a rather unique institution. Comprised of four grade levels, 9-12, and a student body of nearly 400 male-only students, it represented age-old Catholic Jesuit traditions. Each school morning brought an opening morning prayer and the pledge of allegiance followed by announcements. Then the daily class schedule would begin which included Latin, Religion, Math, Science, Social Sciences and Humanities. Overseeing it all were the Jesuit fathers and brothers. They served as administrators, teachers, hall monitors, spiritual advisors, coaches, and disciplinarians. Clad in black robes with a small white square highlighting the starched tight-fitting collar, they were ever present in the passageways and classrooms of the school. Fully understanding the position they were in, the Jesuits attempted to keep a tight lid on any student body mischief or happenstance. Two in particular, Father McDonald and Father McDonough, kept their eyes and ears fully open; they could smell trouble a mile away and took pride in outmaneuvering the cleverest of pranksters. It was a "hide and seek" game: how much questionable behavior could a person get away with before the Fathers stepped in, hack paddles hanging from their cord belts, stern grins easing from their mouths, and then grab your ankles and three quick swats and a return to silent obedience. There were no secret agendas. Either behave or face the likely impact of a piece of carved wood with drilled holes on your back-end.

Alongside the Jesuits were lay teachers and a small group of young men known as Jesuit Volunteers. This latter group of recent college graduates had registered as Conscientious Objectors with the Selective Service Draft Board. They were in opposition to the Vietnam War based on moral principles. In place of military service, they were serving in schools as teachers. With their position came room and board at the Jesuit rectory but little pay, if any. These fellows added a distinctive twist to the overall school setting. Young, charismatic, and wearing fashionable clothes, they seemed to have arisen out of a different age altogether.

There was also the academic side to Bellarmine. The school was a center of advanced learning and scholarship. In one form or another, the totality of students represented a quick-witted, studious, engaged and critical-thinking body. Some of the students came directly from Catholic elementary parish schools, others via experiences in public junior highs, and still others from distant locations unknown. Blended together it was a mixture of brainy intellect, athletic prowess, and street smart adventurism. On top of it all lay a scholastic layer of classics, theology, Socratic dialogue and homework (tons of homework). If one couldn't cut the grade, then there was always the option of seeking another school enrollment. Every so often on a Monday morning there would appear an empty desk, its former occupant gone forth to greener pastures.

As the first weeks of ninth grade progressed, it became obvious that an undercurrent of mirth and merriment lay just below the surface. We had all been on our best behavior in the beginning, listening to classroom rules, taking notes, and attending school-wide assemblies, including one in which selected freshman students were brought up onto the auditorium stage and "initiated" with molasses, flour and other nasty food items. As freshman, we were the underlings. We were assigned a role of low prestige and needed to understand our place in the school especially in the presence of letterman-jacketed seniors. Our day would come, but not for another three years.

Our "D" class homeroom was the center of much interest. I recognized some of the students from north end neighborhoods including one with the idyllic name of Ladd. He came from Mason Junior High and carried himself with a smooth and friendly demeanor. There were others around him similarly amicable and outgoing. It was a welcoming group of peers with many becoming close friends over time. And yet I remember feeling unsettled as if a hammer was about to come crashing through this layer of fun and comradeship. And it did in due time.

It first began with the animal sounds. Students would cuff their mouths with folded hands and let out low vibrating noises of sheep, cows and chickens. I sometimes felt compelled to look out the classroom first floor windows to see if a herd might be meandering by out in the parking lot. Then there were tacks on desk seats, spit wads, wise cracks, fart eruptions, and other general bedevilment. Half of the "D" class would participate in this ongoing behavior and half of the class would sit idly by chuckling and laughing and thoroughly enjoying the ongoing spectacle of humorous delights. It was first-rate spontaneous comedy, born and bred from adolescent male spirits. Maybe this behavior was prevalent due to the fact that there were no females present in the classroom. Unlike most other school experiences, girls were not included in the Bellarmine framework. They were absent, most of the Catholics off across town at two all-girl academies. It definitely changed the atmosphere; no females and all males brought new dimensions to learning and classroom decorum. The Jesuits certainly had their hands full (a fact to which they were well accustomed).

Things came to a head one day in the classroom of a young Jesuit teacher. He had been the target of much misguided "D" student class behavior and was at various moments expressing signs of frustration and impatience. On this particular day, he was attempting to take a class photo, lining us up in the back of the room in two rows, tall kids in the back, short ones in the front. There was obvious resistance, fun and games with students changing places as he would walk back up to his desk to turn around and take the shot. This happened a time or two despite his noted displeasure until he finally couldn't take it any longer. He exploded, racing back to our rows, grabbing an infamous rabble rouser and dragging him by his shirt collar to the front of the classroom and out the door into the hallway. It occurred fast and furious, leaving us stunned, momentarily looking around at each other, surprise and dread in our eyes. At this point no one was laughing. Not a soul. The jokes were over. The game had gone too far. We had pushed a teacher over the edge into blind rage!

Things simmered down in the room after this incident. Administrators were called in to address the problems. We were given strict behavior guidelines and put on warning: no more sarcasm, no more outbursts, no more noise or comments. We experienced a temporary pause and went back to the beginning for a short while, all eyes once again forward and attentive. Soon after, at the end of the first trimester, I was promoted to the "C" class. I recall the day well, walking up the hallway to a neighboring classroom, feeling good about my academic successes but already missing those left behind. I sidestepped a student named Peachy in the hall along the way. We probably looked at each other, heads nodding, both thinking, now what? He was heading down to the "D" class in a case of mistaken identity, spending one day there before being sent back to the "C" class. Later in life, we shared our memories of that time. In his brief "D" class experience, Peachy saw what I saw. He chuckled and squirmed in his seat as I had, he noted the humor and wit and misguided spontaneity. We both agreed: it was a room full of comic geniuses, a precursor to the likes of Saturday Night Live right there at Bellarmine Prep, a classroom of clowns, jesters and mimics all thrown together in gaiety and trouble down at the end of Freshman Hall.

# 13

## The Pirate from Rome

Father Joseph DeJardin was a smallish man with a thin face and sharp nose. His black slightly graying hair lay pinched on top of his head into a fashionable short peak. He would often stand smiling in the front of the classroom, notes in hand, welcoming his students into their seats with a bright "Good morning". He was a happy fellow, energetic and enthusiastic and full of life and knowledge. It was sophomore year at Bellarmine Prep and we were in Father DeJardin's room to learn World History. The school also seemed different; time had moved forward and Bellarmine was undergoing a gradual transformation into a new age. Gone were the "A-D" class divisions and some of the imposed clothes and hair restrictions. It seemed like the school was opening up, letting in a little fresh air, inviting the cultural "winds of change" of the 1960's into traditional Jesuit domains.

During the first week of class, Father DeJardin walked around the

53

room distributing a bundle of paperback novels to each student. As he did so, he informed us that there was not to be a textbook for this class. We were not going to learn world history through the memorization of events and dates. No, such an enterprise would be limiting and redundant. Instead, we would read and discuss fictional accounts of people immersed in history. In our studies, he pronounced, there would be scenes of rousting action, compelling dialogue, intriguing relationships and significant accounts of major historical occurrences. Each book, each novel, would have its own story to tell and its own particular time in history to capture. And we would all follow along, supplementing our shared reading with classroom wall maps, film clips and other reference materials. It was to be an exploration into former times, a search into the legends of lost worlds.

What a great idea, I thought. Could this be for real? We were actually going to study history by reading novels, what Father DeJardin referred to as historical fiction? It seemed too good to be true. As students, we had for years reviewed dense textbooks on geography, catechism and English grammar. We had sat poised in our seats during spelling bees, oral presentations, math computations and, of late, Latin recitations. None of it had felt very adventuresome. Yet, there seemed to be a flicker of hope on the horizon. Reading was to be our guide into the past. And it would be the reading of novels, no less. I couldn't wait to get started.

I had begun active reading at a young age through my mother's inspiration. She loved a good book, particularly mysteries, and would venture to the McCormick Branch of the Tacoma Public library on a frequent basis. We would sometimes join her, siblings and friends, for the quick mile drive up North 26th Street to the Proctor neighborhood. Once in the door of McCormick, she would go her own way, intent on a Sherlock Holmes classic, and we would go ours, scattering throughout the tall shelves of what seemed to be endless book choices. My first interests were Indian fables and sport biographies, including the legendary life stories of Ty Cobb, Bill Russell and Jackie Robinson. Then I found adventure novels, stories of Daniel Boone and Kit Carson and salty pirate tales (*Kidnapped* and *Treasure Island*). Later, I would spend an entire summer engrossed in the planet Mars series of Edgar Rice Burroughs. It was space travel and heroic characters entwined within a red Martian universe far, far away.

It came to be that my varied reading activities increasingly broadened my mind to different places and personalities. There were numerous plot twists, surprise endings, scenes of triumphs and failures, life and death episodes, and many memorable characters striving to survive. I lived in my world knowing there were thousands more held in place along the bright-lit interiors of the McCormick library.

One of the first novels we read in Father DeJardin's class was entitled *The Pirate from Rome*. It was published by Crown Books in 1965 and recounted the story of a Roman citizen named Marcus taken prisoner by the then known "Pirate Brotherhood of the Mediterranean Sea". The year was around 67 B.C. and the cast of characters included Julius Caesar and Spartacus. As the story developed there were descriptions of ship galleys, Roman legionaries, seaborne gladiators and naval battles fought off the Isle of Crete. It was a swashbuckling novel of great intrigue based on true historical events. I couldn't put it down; the story clung to me like a never-ending day dream. I could envision the characters and their fiery tempers. There were arrows flying every which way, spears and swords drawn in hand-to-hand conflict, and Roman senate politics being played out in the background. The book was a world unto itself. It had its own colors, smells and language. I was hooked and lost in my own musings of antiquity.

During the remainder of the school year, we continued to read other novels and discuss related periods of history. It was as if we were traveling on a caravan to remote and exotic places. Along the way we stopped in Scandinavia to learn about the Vikings (*The Long Ships*) and then to Arabia to study nomadic cultures (*The Prince of Omega*) and finally to England and stories of the Round Table and King Arthur. After each book was finished, I wanted to thank Father DeJardin for his thoughtful introductions and commentary. He knew his history and was an educated soul who loved maps, in-class readings, dramatizations and lyrical writing. He was the first truly literary person that I had ever encountered. Even now, forty some years later, I can still recall his voice and demeanor.

Reading as a pastime became for me reading as a passion and eventually the study of literature as a focus in college and graduate school. Nothing made more sense than to view the world through the eyes of intuitive writers. First came the baccalaureate study of American Literature and next Irish Studies (and a Master's degree sojourn in Dublin) and as the years passed personal forays into Pacific Northwest poetry, Slavery and Civil War fiction, Southern literature, and the American West. The music of language kept speaking to me: the words and images and rhythms. And the writers kept writing, bringing forth new settings, varied character encounters, and endless messages and life lessons to be carefully considered and remembered. At each turn, at each concluding chapter, I would seek the next place to sit in a corner chair next to a window, natural light falling upon the pages, to dwell in possibility. Looking back (all the way back to Father DeJardin's room), I gradually came to a profound understanding: I was and still remain a willing lifelong recipient of what the Irish poet Patrick Kavanagh once described as "the true gods of sound and stone and word and tint".

# 14

## Bathing at Lourdes

It started with a train ride southwest from Nice along the Gulf of Lion into the foothills of the Pyrenees Mountains. Mr. Z, a school guide, and I were traveling to Lourdes, in past times a small French market town, and now a Roman Catholic pilgrimage site of visitations and healing waters. What awaited us there was as yet undetermined. I was a leukemia patient looking for hope, seven months into a cycle of chemotherapy. My mother, back home in Tacoma, a gentle being born with deep beliefs and convictions, was a religious devotee praying for a miracle. If the mountain springs of Lourdes could somehow provide deliverance, a resurrection from a formidable disease, then I was willing to bathe in its cleansing pools.

    I too stood as a Roman Catholic, born and raised in church traditions: baptized, confirmed and anointed. I had once served the church as an altar boy, learning the mass in Latin, lighting incense upon the tabernacle of God, secretly attentive to sacred hymns and the teachings of Jesus Christ. Within these experiences, I had felt the wonders and quietness of the church. There had been haunting benedictions and solemn Rosaries and funeral masses and wedding ceremonies and holy days of obligation and purple-draped Good Fridays and flower-celebrated Easters and each year the splendid birth of Christ at Christmas. The notions of faith and charity had entered my being. Like others, I was a young disciple wandering through life dealing mostly with ordinary life affairs. And then, a painful awakening: at age seventeen, a diagnosis of cancer. My eyes widened, we were all unnerved, family and friends, and daily existence seemed a much more frightening endeavor. No wonder when the notion of a summer trip to Europe with Bellarmine students came about, my parents encouraged me to go. But there was one important condition; I must journey to France and visit the Sanctuary of Lourdes.

Upon arrival at the train station, Mr. Z and I set out with backpacks to find the hotel. Lourdes was a hilly town and darkness was slowly falling over its winding streets and small plazas. All the buildings seemed compact and closed in, side by side structures with hanging exterior globe lights and narrow doorways. We walked along a few avenues, Mr. Z asking directions in French, until we came to the hotel, an arched building with square-paned windows. After check-in and a few pleasantries, we ascended a steep stairway into a room with angled ceilings, two beds, a wall mirror, and a bathroom just large enough to turn around in. It was a tight squeeze, toilet, sink and tub, but cozy and sufficient. After freshening up, we went back out into the streets, hoping to find a cheap but tasty restaurant. It was France and Mr. Z was in the mood for escargot and frog legs.

"Do people actually eat these things?" I said to Mr. Z while glancing down at a platter of snails in front of us. I could see a bit of snail still encased in its curved shell, cooling in fragrant juices, as if about ready to crawl across the table. "Of course they do. Just pick up the tongs in front of you, grab the shell and use a small fork to take out the snail. Dip it in the sauce and then into your mouth. You'll love it." I did so and experienced a culinary sensation similar to eating oysters and clams back along Puget Sound beaches. It was soft and juicy and full of tangy flavors. "Not bad," I replied, "I think I'll have another."

As the dinner progressed I lost contact with the tables and conversations around us. There was soup and an entrée followed by cheeses and then coffee and a cherry-flavored dessert. Mr. Z had launched into a description of French chateaux, French art and even a quick table lesson in French history. He himself was a French language teacher, young, hip and brimming with culture. This was not his first trip to Europe nor would it be his last. He knew his way around the hill towns and boulevards of France and was eager to share his knowledge and experiences with me.

After dinner, we went for a stroll up a cobblestone road until we came upon a sparsely lit plaza. Here we were standing in front of a downward sloping mountainside, a rock cave grotto and flowing water its bottom centerpiece. It was the Sanctuary of the Lady of Lourdes, the Blessed Virgin Mary standing within the grotto as a statue in white robes and blue undergarments. Here, long ago in 1858 the Virgin had first appeared to a young French maiden named Bernadette Soubirous, speaking to her with these words:

"I am the Immaculate Conception."

Since that date Mary had made seventeen more reported appearances in the vicinity of Lourdes, instilling peace and grace at each visitation to all witnesses. Then over time and distance arrived news of the miraculous healing properties of the grotto water flowing steadily out of the steep ravines of the neighboring mountain. In due course the pilgrims came, the sick, lame and downtrodden. They flocked to Lourdes to seek enlightenment in front of the grotto and to bathe in its waters. And they were present the evening we stepped forth into the plaza, grouped together in a semi-circle in front of the Blessed Virgin, mostly silent and lost in spiritual meditation. Many were sitting in wooden wheel chairs, some standing supported by crutches or canes, and still others laying full length on medical litters. Amidst the holy ambience and splashing grotto water, I could faintly hear periodic whisperings and prayer words. They were speaking to Mary in hushed tones, awash in her glory and beautiful essence.

The next morning Mr. Z and I awoke to sunshine and golden light. It was the day of my scheduled bath and we ate a quiet breakfast, each of us stoic in our own thoughts. From there, Mr. Z led me to a gate where other pilgrims were lining up to enter the pools. We exchanged parting words, his of encouragement and fortitude, and I watched him walk away back towards the hotel. I was alone then, one amongst others, singular and solitary. Maybe it was the sense of anticipation, of knowing a rare occurrence was about to happen, possibly a transformative life-saving event, that enabled me to close off all hearing and seeing. I stood fixed in place, head down, arms dangling by my sides, gathering myself, awaiting the moment of watery immersion. There seemed to be no others, just me and my own surging emotions.

The line began to move forward propelling us down inside a hallway and changing area, the women stepping to the left and the men to the right. Here we disrobed, placing shoes and clothing in wicker baskets. We were all just skin and bones, elemental beings, meek and humble, caught together in our commonality, each seeking some form of redemption. Wearing only sandals and knee-length grey smocks, we entered an enclosed rock wall passageway within the grotto. It was cold and damp and our movements tight and echoing. One by one we walked forth into a wider room, an alcove, and there lay a rectangular pool, shallow and dark in color. Nearby stood attendants and the administering priest, the one who would say the prayers and ask God for blessings upon us. I watched those in front of me step up, one by one, and be lowered gently backwards into the pool: lower torso first, then head and arms, followed by legs and feet. There they floated, held in place by the attendants, while the priest spoke his holy words in God's language. It may have been French or Latin or possibly even English. Whatever the idiom it was sacred verse intoned in the spirit of healing.

Soon it was my turn to step down into the pool. I slipped off the sandals, turning and easing my way into the water. Looking up, I could see the wet stone walls of the cave enclosure and hear the enunciations of the priest. The water felt chilly yet comforting. I closed my eyes and asked for the forgiveness of my sins, and for a chance, a living chance to grow beyond the disease. I believe God was listening, as was my mother back home, each of them reaching out to pull me from the water, christened, cleansed and cured.

# 15

## T-Town Shuffle

There was an age when driving around in cars was a feat magnificent. Alone or with another, the idea of cruising through town and enjoying the sights was all one could ask for on a given day or evening. At certain moments, there just wasn't much else going on. Known acquaintances might be scattered here and there, out of touch and out of sight, some working, some preoccupied with school and families, and still others beyond the reach of random phone booth calls. So it was fortunate to be able to find a friend and head out, side by side in bucket seats, tunes on the radio, and miles of road in front of us. All one really needed was a suggestion: "Hey, hop in and sit back, it's traveling time. Let's see what lies ahead and what may come of casual conversations and roadside views."

One such friend drove an older, 1950's era Volkswagen Beetle with vented windows. With a cigarette in hand and a story or two to tell, he would stop by the house and off we'd go. Upon leaving Alder Street, we would usually descend 24th Street over the gulch bridge, up and down a short hill to Steele Street and onward towards Lowell School and Aquinas High. On one occasion when stopped at the crosswalk below Lowell, a Stadium High School student came walking across the street carrying a conspicuous pinkish psychedelic record album. We both recognized him as someone a year or two older than us, a friend of friends, his name Kevin or so we believed. He was cool, stepping along, rehearsing the songs of Eric Clapton and Jack Bruce in his mind. He didn't notice us in the car staring at him, following his every move as he headed up the hill towards "I" Street. If he had, we would have smiled, nodding our heads, acknowledging his fine taste in rock music.

Further down Yakima Avenue were old brick apartment buildings and large homes belonging to the well-to-do. The neighborhood was built on expansive hillsides jutting down towards Old Tacoma and Commencement Bay. At every cross street appeared water views and forested headlands in the northern distance ("Look, there's Brown Point straight on and Vashon Island off to the left"). We would often turn onto one of these cobblestone streets until we found our way to the brick-faced exterior of Annie Wright Academy. This place always seemed to shout, "Stay out!" with its sidewalk-fronted hedges and long entrance walkways. It was then and continues today as a private all-girls' boarding school; an institution not for the likes of local townies out on a car jaunt.

From Annie Wright we would turn uphill past the boundaries of the Tacoma Lawn and Tennis Club on the left and a cornerstone brick home on the right. This house had special significance. There was a girl living there sharing the same initials as me, someone I had met and dated early on, and would continue to date through the last chapter of high school and some college years. We had experienced our own rides, the ups and downs of youthful relationships, and were destined for further shake-ups. I thought very highly of this girl, driving by and looking, attempting to catch a fleeting glimpse of her coming out the door or standing by a window. If I knew then what would transpire in future years, I might have whispered to her: "It's all right and good whatever might come to pass. We are who we are, it is what it is, but time will change all things further ahead and we will relinquish our ties and seek new vistas." Whooshing by in the car and looking back, I might also have had one last parting notion: "So maybe it is best now to simply enjoy the time we have together no matter future events. To live in the present might be the answer, our minds clear and at ease, attentive to the beating of our vigorous hearts."

At the top of the street came a quick swing down Borough Lane, past the Club entrance and into a neighborhood known to many as one of bounty and prestige. Here were many families and children, a place centered around a swimming pool and Garfield Park and those spacious tennis courts. The choices were many. Should we stop by and say hello to the Shaws, Leitzingers, Moores, Petrichs, O'Connells, Jacques or Rheas? At times, we would pull over, roll down a window, and look about considering our choices, a tale or two coming forth about friends and circumstances, and then keep on, slowly following a route down past the Museum of History and the awe-inspiring sunken Stadium Bowl. On these occasions, it was more movement and motion than people that fired our spirits. There was much more to see before the day was done or the evening came to a close.

Once past Stadium High the road became a straight descending slope to downtown Tacoma and a favorite stopping point. But first, glancing to the left and over a cliff, there lay the industrial tideflats with smoke billowing out of numerous buildings. This was somewhat of a dreary setting. Here is where the muddy Puyallup River entered Commencement Bay, where giant ships came to load and unload cargo, and where pulp mills like St. Regis and steel works like Fick Foundry held court, oozing chemical vapors into the air and water. It was blue collar, three work shifts per day, union strong and hard labor. Many people in need of gainful employment, young and old, would pass through these factory doors. There were families to be raised, schools to attend, churches to support, and life to be carved out somewhere up above in the intertwining Tacoma neighborhoods. I had come to accept the tideflats area for what it was: jobs, progress and security all huddled together in a smelly, cantankerous, manufacturing human life-hold.

As the hill leveled off near the entrance to downtown, we hung a left-hand turn past the Trailways Bus Depot and into Fireman's Park. Hopping out of the car, we stood and look skyward gazing at the Indian totem pole directly in front of us. It was long and vertical, carved of wood and depicting Native American motifs: a salmon, eagle, raven and near the top, a soaring thunderbird. The totem always stopped me in my tracks, looming there above the watery canals, hinting of times past and the original people who must have lived in Tacoma long before the appearance of white settlers like Ezra Meeker and the emergence of wood mills and steam ships. Climbing back into the car, I would take a little of the totem with me after each visit, its faces and images and colors. Stand tall, it seemed to say, and remember the animals, our guides through life. There are spirits here among us. Stop and listen before moving on.

Our path would continue to wind its way down to the waterfront along hidden downtown byways where snowy Mt. Rainier could sometimes be seen framed within the thrusting 11th Street Bridge turrets, to a bigger road below, out and past the Granary and Sperry Mill (nothing left but water-logged pilings) until we came to Johnny's Seafood and the Old Tacoma Dock. If lucky, we had been running side by side with a freight train to the left, a Northern Pacific or Burlington Northern/Santa Fe, hauling freight in boxcars and maybe lending a ride to a traveling hobo or two. There was tremendous locomotive power in these trains, rumbling along, screeching and whistling, following the shorelines of Puget Sound. Riding parallel to the train, I was ofttimes reminded of American blues' songs, harmonica notes by Paul Butterfield in particular. I would tap my feet, humming the melody to "Two Trains Running" while listening to the click-clack, click-clack repetition of the rails.

Further along the shoreline were other skeletons of wood mills, piers and rocky bulkheads to keep the salt water at bay. There was even a renowned house or two built on stilts over the water and a number of restaurants with outside decks to enhance the populaces' dining pleasure. We were now heading towards the township of Ruston, past the formidable copper smelter and heaps of slag and through the short car tunnel underneath the train tracks. Once out, we turned up a curving hill, slowing a bit, until we came to a blinking street light. Here was Ruston in all its glory: a hardware store, a deli market, a tavern or two, and the local police constabulary lurking around every corner. We were now on Pearl, the main avenue narrowing down into Point Defiance Park. On a bright warm day, it was posing time with automobiles of all makes and models heading to Owen Beach: roasters, convertibles, low-riders, woodies, motorcycles, vans, and sport cars. It was a cop's heyday and a weekend speeding-ticket windfall for the municipality of Ruston.

Once inside the park the road wound past the pond gardens, the zoo cages, and into a deep forested region of firs, cedars and hemlocks. One could then take a right turn down the steep "S" curves to the parking lots above Owen Beach, filled at times with picnickers, boaters, car junkies, and ice cream lovers. On other occasions, the beach would be deserted, inclement weather keeping people at home. We would walk the sandy shoreline, stepping over logs and bull kelp. The place felt like a natural paradise within an urban environment. It smelled of wood, dirt and decomposing sea life. Before climbing back into the car, I would always take one long look out across the water and breathe one last deep breath of refreshing, crusty salt air.

The way out led uphill and onto Five Mile Drive. This was a one-way road free of painted lines with towering trees dominating the landscape. Of all the places in Tacoma, this stretch was the most scenic. I could momentarily feel lost here, surrounded by nature. There were no houses or sidewalks or cumbersome telephone poles, wires branching out in all directions. It was more a tunnel of trees with spaces of open sky at the top, sometimes shimmering blue patches, sometimes passing grey clouds with pelting rain, sometimes both. Further on would come scattered turnouts, places to pull over and enjoy water viewpoints: Dalco Passage, Vashon Island, Gig Harbor and lastly, the towering Narrows Bridge, Tacoma's own Golden Gate but painted green and providing access to places further west like Wollochet Bay, Fox Island and Key Peninsula.

It was at one of these turnouts on a spring weekend that three or four of us broke into a spontaneous dance. We were out of the car, lounging on the cliffside wooden railings and enjoying the fading sunshine when Creedence Clearwater's version of "Proud Mary" came on the radio. Up we stood with our seafarer jeans and suede shoes, a shuffle or two in our step, a full circle twist and turnabout in our walk, bopping and snapping fingers and weaving here and there. It was the music and warmish air that jump-started our bodies like sparks of electric currents tingling up spinal cords. We were loose and carefree. It only lasted a minute or three, but the dance was memorable, a momentary infusion of roadside rhythms.

The last leg took us past Never Land, Fort Nisqually and Camp 6. These were roadside thrills of an earlier age where one could visit with Humpty Dumpty, wander the Fort imagining oneself as a frontiersman, and climb the old logging apparatus at the Camp. On this day, we just kept on driving until we came out of the woods and back to the park entrance. Our final resting place would be the Goldfish Tavern for a schooner of beer and a game of pool. It was time to get out of the car, to see if by chance other friends might be inside enjoying a Saturday evening. For the moment, we had completed our tour, we had seen the sights to be seen, and now we could lean back, thirsty and at ease, into a smoky atmosphere of barroom sway and chatter.

16

The Space Sisters

Haggett Hall sat tucked on a corner hillside overlooking the University of Washington campus and Seattle neighborhoods to the north and east. In the distance were Wedgwood, Laurelhurst and the shores of Lake Washington. Below the twin towers of the dorm, close and within walking distance, one could easily reach University Village, the expansive student parking lots and IMA buildings, and also Husky Stadium, massive and looming, a symbol of the vastness of the UW universe. It was 1973 and time to begin college. My roommate and I were moving into the dorm, floor three, south tower, pentagon-shaped room, long hallways and a shining mirrored bathroom shared by all the male members of our floor unit. I had never lived in a building so large and with so many other people. It seemed like a megahotel or military barracks (disheveled young men in briefs walking the hallways at all hours of night and day). On that first weekend morning, saying good-bye to my mother and watching her drive away in the tan Bel-Air station wagon, I felt a bit out of touch and out of place, a stranger in a strange land, mystified by all that lay before me including the prospect of soon-to-commence college courses.

We spent the first few days exploring the campus and locating our fall quarter classrooms. On the way out of the main entrance of the dorm were silver-sheened compact mailboxes and small lobbies where the elevators were housed. Outside were numerous walkways leading to nearby tennis courts, parking lots and other dormitories. This part of the university seemed like a maze with paths and streets intersecting each other and then meandering off in contrary directions. There was a moment when, suddenly feeling lost, we stepped across a two-lane byway and there before us down a wide set of stairs was a meadow-like area with a strolling lane down the middle and trees bordering each side. It was eye-catchingly beautiful: the perfectly spaced leafy cherry trees, the surrounding ornate stone buildings, and the side pathways branching off to curved doorways and hidden buildings.

"Is this for real?" I said, mostly to myself, muttering the words in quiet disbelief.

In the distance we could see an opening into another area, deeper in texture with a solitary obelisk standing guard, cracked and fractured at the top as if battle-weary and broken. We headed in that direction, down the stairs, past the trees and into the brick-paved area known as Red Square. I had heard the name before in reference to Russian politics and Moscow landscapes but I didn't know such a place existed in Seattle nor there at the epicenter of the University of Washington. It too was impressive, rich in color tones and enclosed by five immense architectural wonders. As we stood in the middle of the square and looked around, I suddenly felt the magnificence of the place: the rising triple towers of Odegaard, the stained-glass windows of Suzzallo, the pillar-columned entrance to Kane Hall, the single castle-like turret of the Administration building, and there looking westward, the watchful statue of George Washington, both hands leaning forward on his sword with the majestic Olympic Mountains rising in the background.

I remember my roommate stating, "This is so cool."

And it was - a university setting of wealth and distinction that neither of us had ever experienced before. One could sense the oldness, the grandeur, the layers of knowledge and wisdom contained within the surrounding structures. It felt good to be standing in such a remarkable place, anticipating our upcoming involvement in academic learning, the classes of Philosophy and Biology to begin on Monday. I remember turning in a circle, taking it all in, and being thankful for the opportunity to be at college, away from home and parents, independent, and looking ahead to greater things to come. It was a feeling of empowerment and satisfaction, a step forward, the opening page of a new episode in an enterprising life.

Heading out of Red Square, we ventured down towards the stadium walking a wide pathway between three-toned brick buildings. Mount Rainier was straight on to the southeast, clear as a bell, and below it a sparkling fountain awaited us, set round with rose gardens and benches scattered about. A few other students and parents were present, passing by and enjoying the sights and sounds of the watery spectacle. We circled the fountain and sat down to relax and collect our thoughts. It had been a momentous weekend and we were waning in energy. A moment or two of quiet reflection was needed and the fountain with its flowering spray provided the perfect setting. So we rested and gazed about for a few minutes, looking but not really seeing, empty of purpose and desire. Time came to a momentary standstill; all movement seemed to pause as if frozen in space - then a blink of an eye, a shuffle of feet and up we stood to make our way back to the dorm. It was time for dinner, the sun lowering in the sky, the basement cafeteria in Haggett already filling up with hundreds of young and famished freshmen.

Of all the meeting places in the dorm, the cafeteria provided the best sightlines for people watching. It was here one could get a true feel for all one's housemates; the hundreds of other students living in Haggett within the two towers and eight floor levels. At the appointed meal hour three times a day, a thundering herd of students descended to the cafeteria via stairways, elevators and outside entrances. There would usually be a line leading into the main doorway, each student grabbing a tray, plate, and silverware, and then proceeding through the buffet selections, filling plates with hot food items, salads, bread, dessert and beverages. When duly fixed with all the dressings of a satisfying meal, the next chore would be to find a table at which to sit. The room was large, airy and noisy with giant rectangular windows looking east. There were many table choices, many places to either hide or welcome the company of others. It was a dilemma; do we reach out to our fellow students, extending a friendly hello, or do we wait sitting separate and alone, biding our time for others to find us?

As it happened, the answer arrived rather unexpectedly and unannounced. After the first two days of sitting here or there at meals engaging in a few table conversations but mostly keeping a low profile, we spotted two female students headed our way through the crowd. We had noticed and commented on them already, the previous evening in fact, having seen them walking side by side in the main lobby upstairs. One was a brilliant blonde with a radiant smile and the other a raven black-haired Asian girl with a quiet infectious laugh. They were quite the twosome: light and dark, gregarious and shy, each beautiful and stylish in her own unique manner. We couldn't help but notice them and now seeing the pair approach our table and quietly sit down right across from us, we were caught off guard, surprised and stunned into momentary silence by our good fortune.

"Hi. I'm Joy," the blonde announced.

"And I'm Marie," the dark-haired girl stated, smiling and reaching out her hand in greeting.

We introduced ourselves and slipped into a casual conversation about class schedules and dorm activities and questions about where we were from.

"Tacoma," I said. "The North end."

"We're from Enumclaw," Joy exclaimed, a friendly grin flashing across her face.

"Hey, we're practically neighbors," replied my roommate.

From there we talked of high schools and scenic points and eventually upcoming weekend plans.

"We actually sat by you guys today on purpose," said Joy. "We picked you out along with a few others to invite to a little party in our room this Saturday night. Would you be interested in coming?"

"We would love to come," I stammered while making eye contact with my roommate and noting his eager affirmative nod.

"Great, see you then," said Marie as she handed me a little invite card with the time and room number cleverly written across the front.

We said our good-byes and watched as the girls returned their trays to the check-out station and left the cafeteria.

Turning and looking back at my roommate, I leaned forward and quietly whispered, "Things are looking up, my friend."

Saturday night arrived with much cheerful anticipation. The first week of classes was in the bank and as there were no pressing concerns, we were feeling light on our feet. With a few beverages in hand, we made our way over to the appointed floor and knocked on the door. Joy answered and invited us in. There were others present, spread out in the room sitting on beds and counters, people we came to know as Jay and Scott and Gary and Bob, all living in Haggett Hall alongside us. Another girl named Susan was also there with curly hair and glasses, an acquaintance from the neighboring McCarty Hall. All together it was a group of nine, a tight squeeze in such a small space. But it didn't seem to matter; everyone was enjoying the camaraderie.

Once settled and introduced, the first thing to catch my attention was the music playing in the background. It was something new, upbeat and jazzy with harmonic vocals. We all had a record player in our rooms and stacks of albums. But this music was something I hadn't heard before. Someone said "What's playing?" and the response was "Steely Dan". Never heard of it, I thought, but it sounds great.

The evening continued with small talk, shared experiences, laughter and commitments to get together soon. We had made a connection, drawn quickly into a friendship group through the efforts of Joy and Marie. They had chosen us amongst many others in the dorm believing we all had something in common - an observed sense of affinity. Maybe it was clothing, hair styles, mannerisms or those first lunchroom table conversations. Somehow they hit the mark. We were off to a good start; all the people in the room seemed to fit together like puzzle pieces. Hopefully, I thought, this might last and there would be additional gatherings ahead.

As it came to pass there were many more moments of rendezvous. From the routine sharing of meals and room visits in Haggett, we branched out to Seattle-area concerts and movies. Then came adventures farther afield including hiking trips to Cape Alava on the Washington coast and Cascade Mountain trails. In one form or another we hung tight, staying friends over that year and into the next three, more often than not keeping in touch or living with each other in houses and apartment complexes. Others were added to the mix, coming and going, friends from past times, most of them from the southern regions of Tacoma and Enumclaw. Some of us stayed in school completing our degrees and some didn't. Some found work more appealing and necessary and others the lure of travel and distant lands. Whatever the circumstances, we had met and bonded in Haggett Hall, young and restless at the time, jump-starting numerous close friendships and romantic affairs.

Joy and Marie came to be known as the Space Sisters. It was a complimentary title, a tribute to their giving natures and free spirits. Without them there would have been no Lance Romance shows at the Rainbow Tavern, no welcoming smiles and early admissions into the Paramount Theatre, no walking the beaches of Santa Barbara, and, most likely, no initial dorm room gatherings in the fall of 1973. They were the social catalyst of a time and place, the conjoiners of a small group of freshmen students, separate and divided yet seeking connections. They opened the door and we all walked in, beneficiaries of their loving grace.

# 17

## The History of Jazz

It was late morning of a cold, misty January day, a Monday, and the beginning of Winter Quarter classes. A small group of us from Haggett Hall had made our way along a winding path under towering fir trees until we came out across a wet lawn leading towards the entrance of the music building. The front doors were wooden and noticeably scarred, heavy to the touch with small squares of inlaid leaded-glass windows and metal handles. At first appearance the doors seemed ancient, an entrance into a fortress filled with history, a past and present thoroughfare of arts and industry. Once inside we found a hive of activity centered within a small lobby containing scattered chairs and couches and a glassed-in reception desk. People were coming and going, students and professors mixing and talking and then suddenly disappearing around corners into hidden rooms. After a moment's hesitation and a quick circular look around to get our bearings, we followed other curious, wayward students down a long hallway to the opening of a small darkly lit auditorium. Stopping and standing silent, I could hear voices and the distinctive sounds of music playing within: horns and piano and the rousing repetitive beats of drums and bass guitar. It was "Music 103: The History of Jazz" with Professor Joe Brazil somewhere on stage, shyly smiling and gesturing, the good-natured man that he was, spinning vinyl for all to hear both inside and out of the classroom.

An awareness of jazz music had begun a few years earlier while I was still a student in high school. Around 1973, in the waning days of the prominent 1960's rock explosion, disco was just beginning its lofty ascent to nightclub fame. There were music fans (myself included) looking askance, wondering what had happened to the soaring abundance of rock and roll vibrations of past times. Our attention naturally turned to favorite musicians and albums that had stood the test of time. There was also a resurgence of the blues, the legendary black American rhythms which had earlier fueled some of the very best British and U.S. rock bands. And in the background, threads and hints of jazz, a mysterious and unknown repertoire of music, splashes of it coming faint across F.M. radio stations, through open car windows, and from stereos in neighboring homes. During those moments, I was hearing jazz notes, the sounds of the music now and again catching my wavering attention, but I really wasn't engaged. It was just occasional background noise, lost below the surface of things.

My own jazz awakening occurred during a late summer's day sojourn. It was a warm afternoon with the windows open and soft breezes pushing and pulling the curtains in and out the room. A friend had stopped by, albums in hand, to spend a little time catching up and listening to tunes. He happened to have a jazz album in the stack, a Les McCann and Eddie Harris live recording from Montreux, Switzerland. We put it on, first wiping and cleaning the record to remove any fine dust, and sat back to enjoy the music. The first song hit me straight on, the opening rolling piano line with drum and bass backups (applause) followed by rising horns and the rich vocals of Les McCann. It was a soulful jazz composition with a protest message, lyrics about troubled times and "trying to make it real compared to what". I was captured, drawn into the depth and complexity of the music, the layers of instruments one on top of the other, connecting and thriving and then drifting off, the sax and piano and trumpet, only to come back again with each instrument then taking center stage, clear, decisive and clairvoyant. So this is jazz, I thought, music so striking and powerful in texture and tone. What could be next, I wondered as the first tune ended and there was a momentary pause, the record still in motion, the needle finding its way to the second song. Up came "Cold Duck Time", a gradually soaring composition featuring Eddie Harris on sax. There were moments of passion in this composition, an interplay of instruments leading to rising crescendos. The sax sounds were potent, searing and at times screeching yet coming clear and forceful from within Eddie Harris's creative persona. It was music with unusual depth; one had to focus, to lay aside distracting thoughts, to be able to follow the curves and twists of all the instruments. And holding it together, Les McCann playing stellar piano, lyrical and twinkling and star-bright, beautifully interwoven in all of the album's compositions, sometimes leading the way, solo and up front, and sometimes in the background, adding pristine notes like a flowing, coursing river in a canyon of sound.

This jazz moment led to others, an active exploration of the genre through affiliations and associations. When possible, I would peruse album collections of older brothers and friends, hoping to discover hidden jazz artists, similar to searching for agates on a beach of rocky outcroppings. In record stores, I would stroll past the captivating sections of Blues and Rock until I found Jazz A-Z, smaller in volume, yet stocked with names then known and unknown. I would stop and read the back of album covers to learn the history of the music, the recording dates, the personnel and the reviews. Over time, I picked up a record or two, Herbie Hancock, Miles Davis, and Monk, which opened my eyes even further into the foundations of jazz. This music had been present for a long time, in different variations and evolutions, an important vein of culture within society, composed and orchestrated by artistic giants. Feeling famished, I was hungry for more. Soon, this need, this personal desire to discover jazz in greater scope, brought me to the moment of anticipation outside the Music 103 auditorium, the currents of jazz escaping into the hallway, and myself, suspended in place, turning and entering the darkened room.

The lights were low and the music was coming from a portable stereo system onstage. There sat Joe Brazil, a small, older man with a thin grayish beard wearing a red African skull cap, sitting in a desk chair alongside the stereo, organizing his notes and arranging albums. I came to learn he was originally from Detroit, an accomplished sax and flute player himself, an early friend and musical colleague of John Coltrane. Joe had come to Seattle in 1961 to work for the Boeing Company, bringing his instinctive flair for jazz along with him. This led to teaching opportunities at Garfield High School and the founding of the Black Academy of Music in Seattle. He came to the University of Washington as an adjunct professor partly due to the insistent demands of the UW Black Student Union; here was a brilliant jazz gem right in our midst, a notable recording artist, making Seattle his home and jazz theater. They decided to add him to the faculty of the music department for the benefit of their aspiring students.

Joe would always start class with prolonged minutes of music. Students would come shuffling in, cold and often soggy from the mist and rain, finding seats and folding back comfortably into baggy warm sweaters and hats. The jazz would be waiting for them, drifting and floating and filling the space with poetic harmonies. After a few opening songs, Joe would begin his lectures, interspersing historical jazz facts with personal antidotes and musical selections. Each class day brought widened perspectives: new artists, new knowledge, new exposures to jazz times and ventures. Joe had a unique way of pulling you into the music, the personalities, the rise and fall of jazz legends. His voice was sure and soft and the music well-scripted and enlightening. On certain days, visiting jazz artists would show up for class, sitting and playing with Joe on stage, those who happened to be in town engaged in concerts or night club shows. These were surprise appearances, unknown beforehand to the students, but special in spontaneity and musical composition. There would be Clark Terry on trumpet or Roy Ayers on vibraphone, the small auditorium itself becoming a jazz recital hall. Between songs, brief discussions would take place, Joe and guest talking jazz lingo and taking questions from the students. Then into another song, another jazz phrase, jazz cycle, jazz rhythm, pulling us forever deeper into the intricacies of the music.

On one memorable day, I walked into class and was introduced to Eddie Harris. He was greeting students with Joe, shaking hands and enjoying a cup of coffee. Before long he fired up his saxophone and launched into an extended solo. It was all electrically amplified, pumped up and far out and remarkable. He was exploring musical spaces I hadn't heard before, soaring to even greater heights than those found with Les McCann on "Swiss Movement". Eddie was in his element that day, immersed in his own jazz designs, with Joe Brazil as his channel and the students his transfixed audience. The melodies were caught in time, dancing from within the auditorium out into the hallways of the music building, finding others held in place, suspended like myself in musical rapture.

# 18

## The Green-Eyed Monster

"As a jealous man I suffer four times over: because I am jealous, because I blame myself for being so, because I fear that my jealousy will wound the other, because I allow myself to be subject to a banality; I suffer from being excluded, from being aggressive, from being crazy, and from being common."

Roland Barthes

The beginning of the end took place one evening at a birthday celebration on University Avenue. We were all gathered together in a downstairs restaurant at the end of a school day to raise a toast to a roommate turning twenty-two years of age. It was a planned social affair with most of the invited guests in attendance, old and new friends alike, culminating in a festive atmosphere of "eat, drink and be merry". My girlfriend was also at the table, somewhat newly arrived in Seattle as a transfer student at the University of Washington. She had enrolled for Fall Quarter after spending a few years going to school out of state. For us it was a rekindling of a relationship that had been born in the late middle school years, burning bright during high school, and then flaring hot and cold during college and repeated lengthy separations. Yet there we were together, side by side, united once again, a bit older in age and experience but definitely determined to make a go of it. Or so I thought.

At one point in the evening she excused herself to find a restroom. Taking her coat and purse along with her, I knew she was heading up to the main street level commons where the public bathrooms were located. After what seemed a long period of time, I began to sense her absence. Troubling thoughts ran through my mind. Was she safe? Did something happen? Maybe she was not feeling well, possibly sick from the food and drink? Prior to this moment, she had been struggling with all the recent changes in her life. She seemed to be caught in a confusing transitional state, dealing with a relocation, a different university setting, a larger city, important school decisions regarding majors and educational directions, and possibly, our own renewed relationship. It had not been an easy chapter for her, coming to Seattle and getting anchored. I had attempted to stand with her and provide support and encouragement. I had also found my feelings for her growing stronger and deeper. I was happy she was in town, happy that we were given this chance to find each other again.

I left the group and walked up the stairs to check on her. At the upper doorway leading into the commons, I stopped mid-step seeing out of the corner of my eye a phone booth. There she was in an animated conversation, smiling within the tall glassed-in space, her voice muffled and hidden, moving the phone from one ear to the next, all aglow with a rosy complexion. My first thought was that I hadn't seen her this happy in a long while. Something good had happened. She must be talking to a family member. However, as I stood there watching and waiting, a gradual sensation of uncertainty slowly enveloped me. It started in my feet and rose vibrating up through my chest and arms landing complete and steadfast in my brain. I tried to shake it off, to get a grip, to find a hold on things. I soon found myself locked in place, the uncertainty blanketed by rising emotions of dread and panic. It wasn't a family member she was talking to, I thought. It was someone else, unknown to me, a person she obviously cared for, maybe, just maybe a possible rival.

I thought I knew this girl well. We had grown up together, so to speak, taken many youthful steps in tandem, finding common paths and adventures to share with each other. I had through time learned to read her facial expressions, to sense the hopes and fears glittering in her eyes, and to know when to give her space, to leave her quiet with her own thoughts, and when to be beside her, a friend and more. So when she stepped out of the phone booth and saw me standing there, it was a moment of recognition. All past common episodes flashed instantly before us, come and gone in a brief second or two like a super fast-forwarded movie script. Then it was over, we blinked and it was real time. She suddenly moved to the outside door, to leave, to flee, to travel on her way. I stopped her, held her in place momentarily asking her what was going on, who was she talking to, what was the matter? Her response was a request to leave her alone, to let her go, to stand aside, to not block her way. We both pushed through the doors and out onto the sidewalk together. I was a step behind and in pursuit, stumbling and blinded by confusion. She kept going, walking quickly down University Avenue, the night growing darker around us, her back to me and her feet bound for destinations unknown. I followed, imploring her to stop, to turn around and talk with me. She didn't. She just moved away even faster, taking a left turn onto a side street and walking onto campus under the dim lights of lamps and the shadows of trees. I let her go and began my own solitary walk back to the birthday gathering, to waiting friends, and the celebration of age and another year come and gone.

I didn't hear from her for a while: a few days, a week, or possibly a little longer. Nor did I reach out to her. I was stunned into silence by my own riotous emotions. From the moment we separated on University Avenue, I began spiraling down into a state of tension and anxiety. I felt neglected, wounded, angry, and suspicious. What would be the point of talking to her? I had seen the truth of the matter in her actions, I had heard the sounds of dismissal in her words. I was left alone, residing privately with my own personal demons, caught in the grip of jealousy, the green-eyed monster always lurking hidden and sorrowful within heartfelt relationships, raising its ugly head at moments such as this, sneering and wreaking havoc. The emotional descent took me to realms I hadn't been before. I was shaken by anguish, insecurity, and possessiveness. Around and around my emotions churned and turned like a nonstop rotating Ferris wheel. I wanted to get off but couldn't. I was trapped in a cycle of abandoned misery.

One night, well into the late evening hours, she appeared outside my bedroom window, tap, tap, tapping on the pane. I could see her silhouette, part in light, part in darkness, whispering to me to let her in. I hesitated, wavered, unsure of the right thing to do. Yet, my needs proved overwhelming. I wanted to see her, to speak to her, to hold her and pretend that all might be good and right no matter recent experiences. I wanted to forgive and forget, to move forward, to set things straight. I still needed her. Even amidst my bitter feelings of betrayal, I still wanted her. So I let her in. Few words were actually said, it was late and beyond the hours of coherent explanation or easy reconciliation. We just folded into each other, secure in remembrance and affection until sleep played its part. In the morning, she was gone, a lingering ghost slightly present in the room, her smell, her touch, and her few words, soft and empty, floating silently away.

The last time I saw her was on campus. I was standing on the steps of Smith Hall looking out across the rows of cherry trees. It was a winter day, cold but clear, with rays of sunshine striking the brick faces of nearby campus buildings. There were many students coming and going that afternoon, books in hand, quietly passing on the way to classrooms and dorms. I may have been waiting for her, hoping to see her, believing she was coming to meet me. I was still transfixed in hope and self-preservation. And then there she was, walking down the middle path towards Red Square with another, seemingly oblivious to the world around her. I found myself moving down the steps to intercept them. It was only a minute or two and there we were standing together, being introduced and shaking hands, her newfound love, and my antagonist. I held my tongue. I felt the closeness between them, the eye movements, the easy caresses, and the lightheartedness of their interactions. I followed along, down past Odegaard Library and off campus, one street leading to another until we came to the Last Exit Cafe. We went inside and sat at a table together relishing in the warmth and coffee. The conversation was of routine things: courses, midterms, favorite professors, and campus events. We did not talk of each other: of loves lost and found, of present roles and past relationships, and of feelings held in check yet running deep and sacred. No, we just maneuvered around each other, tiptoeing through the tulips, no one speaking the truth of things. It was there and then that I had a realization: the separation was complete, there would be no going back. She was now in a different universe, one she had chosen and most likely needed, and I was not in the script. So I stood up, said my good-byes and headed out the door. There were no spoken protests ("wait, don't go"), no last minute reconsiderations, just a friendly departure and a long thoughtful walk home up Brooklyn Street.

At the end of the academic quarter, I withdrew from the university, loaded up my backpack and headed out of town with old friends. It was the beginning of a five-month road trip south to California via the beaches of the Oregon Coast, east along Interstate 40 to Virginia Beach, then south again to Florida and finally a summer work layover in New Orleans. I was in search of separation, of miles and miles of distance between myself and everything said and not said in Seattle. Along the way I thought of many things: loss and loneliness, hope and endurance, inconstant love, and my own surging need of family. But mostly, I was traveling through time, listening to the wheels on the road, and summing up my own emotions. Where did all these feelings come from, why so strong and lasting? It was the nature of duplicity that eventually held my attention. How could I feel so rational one moment and irrational the next? How could I remain so mature and restored on a given day only to fall crashing headlong into infantile bouts of pity and jealousy? It was a puzzle without a clear set of answers. But the road was up ahead and there was time to figure things out. I just kept my eyes on the horizon, letting the passing landscapes furnish me with new and promising visions.

# 19

## Southern Matters

I spent the summer months of 1977 washing dishes in a cramped upper-story kitchen in the historic French Quarter district of New Orleans. Both inside and out the air was humid, moist to the touch, like a wet blanket enveloping the body. At first the climate was difficult to endure. My breathing would catch now and then in my throat, the vaporous moisture choking the air, while around me, exhaling as if a creature rising from the depths of a nearby bayou, were the noises and sensations of the tropical environment: the lingering sweat, smells and tastes of fecund New Orleans. I felt transported to a distant world, one in which water haunted a submerged land, and all things dripped with liquid elegance.

At the time, I was a college student officially withdrawn from school, on leave, so to speak, but still determined to complete an English degree in the upcoming academic year. New Orleans was part of a respite, a cross-country road trip interval with friends which had begun in April and carried forth across mountains, deserts, canyons and sweeping plains until we arrived at the Atlantic coast and then south to the Gulf of Mexico. There were also family members in New Orleans, two older brothers, one just finishing law school, and the other a medical resident off somewhere in the Louisiana townships administrating to the sick and feeble. It was at his house that we stayed, a renovated former slave quarters behind a large home. It couldn't have been better timing for two wandering college students with little money and thousands of road-weary miles behind them. There was a place to dwell rent free, jobs to be had in the restaurant industry, a family guide close by, and the heat-inflamed mysteries of New Orleans before us.

The French Quarter turned out to be a gold mine of galleries, music joints and southern cuisine cafes. It was here I first discovered voodoo worship, amulets, charms and spiritual dolls dangling from interior walls of back lane shops. Going further into the depths of the Quarter, one could find hidden treasures around every corner: ethnic eateries, small fancy hotels, street musicians, sleazy bars, jazz clubs and lots of people mixing and mingling, many of them enjoying the casual openness of the Big Easy with take-it-to-go flavored beverages. No matter the time of day or night, there was movement in the Quarter, a constant stirring of tourists and locals thrown together in a place that never seemed to sleep. Add in the steamy hot weather, the flammable mix of spicy food and strong alcohol, and one had a gumbo of vibrant humanity: alive, feverish, and ever so close to boiling over.

On one of my outings through the Quarter, I discovered a reclusive and somewhat decrepit used bookstore. I happened to come across it by accident. One minute I was walking along eyes forward and alert and the next moment I was looking through its dusty, grease-smeared windows at rows and rows of stacked books. Upon entering, a bell jingled from above the door, and an older woman appeared at a counter surrounded by papers and piles of books yet to be shelved. She gave me a warm welcoming smile and asked if I needed help finding anything in particular.

"Literature," I responded.

"I'll show you the way," she said and led me down an aisle to the section with "Fiction" on the right and "Literary Criticism" on the left.

"And around the corner is 'Drama and Poetry'," she stated while pointing to the back of the store.

I was looking for Southern literature, intent on finding writers from this region of the nation's broad canvas. I had few ideas in mind. I had been introduced to one or two Southern novels here and there in college and high school but had only truly spent considerable time exploring Thomas Wolfe, a novelist from North Carolina. Wolfe had been an early discovery; my New Orleans brother James and I both shared a coming-of-age interest in his writing talents. Wolfe was a wordy, expressive literary giant of prose fiction who wrote expansive autobiographical-laced novels of youth and separation. *Look Homeward, Angel,* the story of Eugene Gant, had been a mesmerizing read, leading to other continuation novels (*Of Time and the River* and *You Can't Go Home Again*). On the way across country, my traveling companion and I had stopped in Asheville, North Carolina to visit his family home. It was a tree-shaded Victorian structure that once served in real life as a boarding house owned and operated by his mother Julia. As a setting, it came to prominence in his fiction, aptly named Dixieland and full of diverse and colorful characters.

Beyond Wolfe, there really wasn't much else. Vague memories of a Tennessee Williams play, a single Faulkner novel, and a short story by Flannery O'Connor came to mind as I stood silently staring at the book spines along the shelves. I was hungry for more and began searching. Before long, I came across a hard copy edition of *The Circus in the Attic,* a collection of short story fiction by Robert Penn Warren. I knew little about him but read on the inner book sleeves that he was from Kentucky. There was also information on the front cover stating he was the "author of the Pulitzer Prize-winning novel, *ALL THE KING'S MEN*". This will do just fine, I thought, and paid and left the store, heading back towards the intersection of Bourbon and St. Louis and the beginning of my work swing shift in the upstairs kitchen.

Warren turned out to be a godsend. The book was comprised of fifteen stories, mostly short in duration, with the title piece much longer, an imaginative and compelling life history of a boy in a riverside southern town residing at home, caring for a sick mother, and escaping at night into an attic to carve and paint circus animals. Warren's writing was musical with long narrative sentences and poetic word combinations. In the late mornings, I would wake up in the slave quarters, open the window shades, and read for an hour or more before joining the world. Warren was describing part and parcel the southern culture I was experiencing: the river banks, shotgun houses, Baptist churches, the great oak and tulip trees and

85

the people, many of them surviving day by day as best they could. Upon completing the book one afternoon while riding the St. Charles streetcar into town, I immediately walked back to the bookstore and acquired the other Warren novel I had seen resting on the shelves. I soon learned this one would be about Willie Stark and Louisiana politics and intrigue.

So I disappeared into *All the King's Men*, all six-hundred plus pages of it, while sometimes sitting in Jackson Square, or on a bench overlooking the Mississippi River, or riding the street cars to and from Canal Street, or on a rainy day, relaxing inside Café du Monde sipping rich brown chicory coffee and eating sugary beignets. The language and story of the book held me captive: the tumultuous rise and fall of the thinly disguised Huey "Kingfish" Long and the keen philosophizing and awareness of the book's narrator, Jack Burden. It was a human story of corruption and power, set in the Deep South amidst bright sunshine, court houses and fat politicians in striped pants and big cars.

The experience of reading Robert Penn Warren served to further cement my goal of completing an English degree. At moments, I would look up from my reading and stare into empty space envisioning my own circumstances. I would drift back to Seattle and the University of Washington and recall lectures and class discussions and essay papers I had written both memorable and not. I had chosen the study of literature after dallying in Journalism and Political Science because it had intrigued me the most. It was again the life within books which had aroused my greatest attention: the characters, settings, plots, and surprising interactions. Warren reassured me that there was a formidable core of knowledge and insight to be found in literature and in contemplative reading and lyrical language. His storytelling and verse-writing were an inspiration, his re-creation of southern moods a direct link to my summer experiences in New Orleans.

In late August, three of us began a journey back to the Pacific Northwest: myself and my traveling friend to reenroll in school, and older brother James to begin a law clerkship in Tacoma. We were leaving behind the humid air of the Gulf and heading north towards mountains, fir trees and cooler skies. In my backpack, I had brought along another southern novel to help ease the many miles ahead, a book also purchased from what was then and will remain forever my favorite bookstore in New Orleans. *Light in August*, it was entitled, a William Faulkner masterpiece, the haunting story of Joe Christmas and Lena Grove and their shared saga of race, class and troubled ancestry.

# 20

## Irish Chapters

There must have been a day, possibly an early morning, when Owen and Mary Galligan stepped outside their dirt floor hovel in Leinster and, standing arm in arm, decided it was time to go, to leave Ireland once and for all. The air around them would have been moist and breezy with sunbeams piercing downward through the clouds, and in the distance beyond the neighboring small homesteads, the sights of lush green hillsides awakening in the dawn light. Both Owen and Mary were born and bred in County Meath, near the Hill of Tara, a once sacred seat of the High King of Ireland. The children of poor tenant farmers, they too were attempting in their new marriage to carve out a decent life on a small patch of land, growing potatoes in thin strips and hoping to secure a pig to boost their meager possessions. Like all the others around them, they were leasing land from English or Anglo-Irish landlords, stuck in a relentless cycle of rural impoverishment and destitution. Being Catholics, they were also denied basic religious and educational rights, all possibility of wealth and advancement hindered by British laws. As the toils of another day were about to begin they stood and looked into the future and saw little promise. It was then Mary vowed her children would attend school and learn to read and write, an opportunity neither she nor Owen ever had.

Soon after, sometime in the year 1837, Owen and Mary bundled together their meager belongings and traveled to Dublin by rail. There they made their way down to where the River Liffey emptied into Dublin Bay, past the Custom House and Georgian mansions, eventually landing amongst the storehouses and quays of the flourishing city. They had booked a cheap, 3000-mile passage on a ship headed across the Atlantic Ocean to New York City. It was to be a one to two-month crossing, living below decks in a crowded cargo hold with other emigrant Irish. By the 1830's, five thousand native-born Irish men, women and children were leaving the island each year destined for American and Canadian cities (and this before the great Irish Famine laid waste to the country in the 1840's). In tall wooden sailing ships they would heave and ho through gales and heavy seas often burdened by hunger and disease. There was enforced water rationing and a scant pound of food per day for each person with occasional moments up on deck in calmer waters to breathe fresh air, wash clothing and clean themselves. It was a dangerous voyage and not one survived by all the passengers.

✢

More than a century and four generations later, I walked into a "History of Ireland" class on the first day of my last academic quarter at the University of Washington. There were many things to be learned about my ancestral country that I didn't know. I was aware that my last name had Irish tones and that the Catholic faith was steadfast within my family. I once wore the satin green uniforms of St. Patrick's School and learned the Mass in both Latin and English. But there was little else: no remembrance of grandparents, no embellished family history, no Irish songs or jigs, just a nod or two on March 17th while watching others drink green beer. Mine was an American upbringing through and through, a toast to the new world, where progress and opportunity were beacons of light burning brightly.

✢

Upon landing in New York City, Mary and Owen did not receive a hero's welcome. They settled in drab temporary lodgings close to the south side seaport and began looking for work. There was not much to be found. The surge of poor and diseased Irish immigrants into New York harbor was not a comforting sight. As they walked the wharves and piers, nearly penniless, Owen and Mary were frowned upon by homegrown New Yorkers, seen as intruders competing for jobs that were few and far between. Wherever they turned, insults and hostility were waiting as well as posted signs in most street front windows: "No Irish Need Apply". It was a time of perseverance, expectation and lingering hopelessness. With no work at hand, they turned their sights outward, beyond the confines of New York City towards Pennsylvania and the ore-rich coal mines of Pottsville.

✢

My Irish history class was led by a young professor just getting his feet wet in the vast academic circles of UW. He was following in the footsteps of a more famous lecturer, the renowned Giovanni Costigan whose publication, *A History of Modern Ireland, with a Sketch of Earlier Times* was to be the class textbook. If enthusiasm might be considered one of the inspirations of stellar teaching, this professor was standing head and shoulders above many others I had encountered in my baccalaureate studies. He was present and eagerly waiting in the classroom each morning before students arrived, greeting each one as they came in the door, soon learning many names and establishing a mentor-like presence as he stood up front welcoming us with a broad smile and casual conversations. His love of Irish history was ever evident: he was knowledgeable, verbose and enraptured by his own teaching merits. He would at times lean over the front row of seats, looking out upon the faces in the classroom, making eye contact, his voice raising with exclamation, until we were held in suspension, awaiting the final lines, his singular points of contention concerning all that had gone amiss in Irish politics and religion. We soon learned that Irish history was one ripe with subjugation, colonization, confiscation and waves of emigration. There were the original people of Eireann and their circular stone raths, followed by a thousand-year insurgence of Celtic Gaels arriving from neighboring Europe (giving Ireland a common culture, language and religion), and then over the passing of time and history, countless invaders from across the seas, beginning with the Norsemen who sacked and pillaged Celtic monastic centers and schools, all but eliminating the art of illuminated manuscripts. Up rose the Round Towers, then and now cylinder-stone symbols of refuge, where whole villages would seek escape from the river-borne wild-haired men in long ships. But this was only the beginning. In due course would follow the Norman Knights, the Tudors and finally eventual total British domination from Cromwell all the way to partial island independence, the Irish Republic in 1922.

I came to see Irish history as one of exile and sorrow. There were conquerors, famines, Penal Laws, poor houses, ruling classes, peasant evictions and years upon years of English supremacy. The native people, mixed and born and bred on land more pastoral than agricultural, were close to the earth, living on seashores and river banks and within bog-filled valleys, meadows and grazing pastures surrounded by luminous mountains. Within these people there seemed to be a firmness of will not only to live and survive, but to overcome adversity in all its cruel forms. At each downward turn, the loss of life, the loss of land and religious practices, they would rebound with renewed vigor led by such formidable heroes as Brian Boru, Wolfe Tone, Robert Emmet, Daniel O'Connell, Charles Parnell and Patrick Pearse. There were many issues worth fighting and dying for, the quest for liberty the most sustaining. The bells would ring for freedom intoning such causes as the Fenian Movement, Catholic Emancipation, the Gaelic League, Home Rule, Sinn Fein, and the Easter Rising. These causes and more, those heroes and many like them within the faithful and loyal, would eventually lead Ireland into autonomy, modernity and rising prosperity.

✢

Owen and Mary lived and worked in the Pottsville, Pennsylvania region for nearly ten years, bringing into the fold four children, the eldest a son named Patrick followed by three daughters (Bridget, Katherine and Mary). It was a humble life with Owen employed as a miner, descending into the dark and forbidding pits to hammer and claw at broken walls in search of carbonaceous seams. There were injuries and deaths in the mines on an almost daily basis and little money to show for such arduous labor. Yet they endured; living simply, raising children, resting and attending church services on Sunday, somehow avoiding catastrophe illnesses and life-threatening mining accidents. In time, they came to hear of fertile farm lands to be had for easy money in the southwestern Wisconsin territory. This was music to their ears, a chance to be reunited with the earth, to dig and plow and sow a land more rich and fruitful than that once tenured in Ireland. So again, they bundled together their few possessions and headed in search of better places.

Their travels took them west through Ohio and Indiana and then north up to Chicago where they disembarked at the central train depot awaiting a transfer for the final journey into southern Wisconsin. Their destination would be Elk Grove, not far from the Illinois border, an area already familiar to Irish immigrants, where small clay dirt mines and scattered farmlands were abundant. Here they settled amidst log cabin churches and storefronts, clapboard houses and sod-fenced farms. They cleared their own land and endured the hardships and privations of frontier life. Two more children were born, Andrew and Christopher, making it a family of eight. For amusement there were parties and barn dances, shooting matches, horse races, and harvest celebrations. Owen and Mary made a permanent life for themselves in Lafayette County, Irish-born and American-stamped, becoming long-term beloved community members until their separate deaths and burials. Their descendants grew in number and longevity with each forthcoming generation moving a little further west, first into Iowa and then across state lines into Minnesota and finally onward to the shores of Puget Sound. From the offspring of Owen and Mary came multiple families, numerous cousins, engagements and weddings, births and baptisms, and children upon children still carrying forth the Galagan legacy. Looking back, I count my own successions: Owen begat Andrew who begat Robert who begat Cyril who begat Joseph who begat Kevin and Sean. From the tumultuous toils of Ireland a family ancestry was made and transported to the new world. Like most life histories, it was all for the better and for the worse, for the good times and the bad, for what was earned and lost and for what at times was heartwarming and at times saddening. It was and remains a replenishing story and bloodline.

✢

During the last weeks of winter quarter, past the taking of mid-term exams and before my last essay paper was due, I ventured over to visit my Irish History professor in his office. I had a few questions for him. By this time, my interests in Ireland were peaking; the geography, politics and characteristics of the Irish people had caught my attention. And so had the literature. I had read some Joyce and Yeats in previous English courses and had seen a compelling local Seattle production of a Sean O'Casey play. In my mind, I was pondering the idea of a travel visit to Ireland connected to a summer academic course or workshop. Might this professor know of a program? He himself had studied in Ireland and seemed a likely source of information. A few minutes into the conversation, when he learned I was an English major soon to complete my degree, his eyes opened wider and brighter and he asked whether I had ever heard of University College Dublin.

"I have not," I stated.

"You are a talented student full of questions and ideas. You have added to the class, you have been a willing participant, responsive and engaged. And you have expressed a passion for literature," he responded.

His words were kind and considerate. It felt like an unexpected positive affirmation of all the work and time that I had given not only to the Irish History class but to the past four plus years of English studies.

"Might you consider a Master's Program in Ireland?" he continued. "You have the abilities to go further with your studies. And there are worthy programs in Dublin either at the Catholic University or Trinity College."

Sitting there across the desk from this benevolent professor, listening and quietly contemplating his words and suggestions, a distinct but plausible idea began to take immediate shape in my brain. He had planted the seed and added a dose of encouragement. That was all I needed to envision a sojourn in Ireland involving a graduate program and advanced coursework in Irish Literature.

"Thank you sir, I greatly appreciate your words. Your belief in my academic abilities means a lot to me. I will definitely look into the matter. Good-bye and see you tomorrow in class."

With that we both stood up and shook hands. It was a passing moment but one filled with meaning and conveyance. He had given me a gift, a tangible objective, an idea filled with exciting prospects. On my way down the stairs and out of the building, I felt like I was floating above ground, my heart racing and my mind turning over and over with possibilities. Ireland was there before me: the land, the history, the saints and the scholars, and my ancestors, those who had forged a path long ago leading to this notable moment in time.

# 21

## To the Edge of Inishmore

I left for Ireland on a warm day in late August 1978. The week before had been a whirlwind of activities: travel confirmations, packing for an extended year-long stay, visits with friends, and the night prior to departure, a final meal with parents and family, all of us sitting around the dining room table enjoying a fine meat and potatoes feast and relishing each other's company. I remember the occasion well: the toasts of luck and good fortune, the promises of correspondence, a special card my mother had handed me full of blessings and kindness, and there beside me a newfound other, a woman I had met that summer, someone full of life and sincerity, someone I was growing closer to with each passing moment. Her name was Katherine and she had first appeared at a lunch gathering, tall and unassuming with a welcoming smile and keen intelligence. We had spent the past few months together learning about one another and attending movie events, theater productions and making weekend journeys to parks and zoos all eventually leading to this farewell sendoff dinner. I would be the first of my generation to journey back to the old country. That fact was evident before us. A turning of the tide had begun with winds blowing east to the shores of Europe. It was almost time to go, to find what my mother had described in her card as the "roots of home".

The beginning of my travels turned out to be wearisome. First came the long plane flight from Seattle to London, followed by underground tube rides to a rail station where I booked a ticket to Holyhead on the coast of Wales in the Anglesey region. From there I would venture by ferry across the Irish Sea to a port town named Dun Laoghaire just south of Dublin. I had brought along too much luggage so at various stops I discarded items to lessen the burdensome load. A cheap portable typewriter was left in an open locker, a few weighty and unnecessary books deposited near communal benches, and two or three items of heavy clothing including a winter coat I folded and tucked below an empty seat on the train taking me eastward to the ferry landing. All through the prolonged hours of traveling as I made my way from one departure point to another, I was feeling a bit edgy. Sleep would not come in any shape or form and as time progressed and I sat quietly waiting in stations staring blankly into space, I began to wonder if I had made the right decision. Fatigue was wearing me down, playing tricks with my mental state, causing me to lose purpose and drift into uncertainty and disillusionment. Luckily, the ferry provided an opportunity to go outside and breathe ocean air. I walked beside the outer railings engulfed by the wind, my hair and clothes flapping about, and then stopped and stood looking out into the distance towards Ireland, feeling refreshed and finding once again the strength to carry on. I was alone but not deterred. I was on the brink of wakefulness, bone-tired, but determined in mind and spirit.

Upon landing in Dun Laoghaire, I descended from the ferry with the rest of the walk-on passengers into a waiting room lobby. People were coming and going, jumping into buses, cars and taxis, everyone seemingly headed for preordained destinations. I glimpsed all this while resting on a chair and looking out a window into the early morning rising light. There were trees and a field beyond the paved loading zones and in the trees were birds flitting about, chasing one another in a circle of play and merriment. While watching the birds, I soon became mesmerized by their movements and unaware of all other actions around me. Half asleep, half awake, passing in and out of slumber, I slipped into a dreamlike state where consciousness folded into reverie, light into twilight, and all aspects of present time paled beyond recognition. I had arrived in Ireland and become adrift only a few feet away from shore. And there I stayed for minutes or more, not long but seemingly longer, until a call went out for anyone needing a taxi. I awoke, the moment at hand, suddenly aware of my need to find a way into Dublin.

"I do," I half shouted, picking up my baggage and belongings.
"Right man, where to?" came the reply.
"The Kennedy Hotel."

✢

I slept for nearly 24 hours once I was secured and under the covers at Kennedy's. The place had been recommended by my parents, a hotel close to downtown with reasonable rates and comfortable beds. After check-in, I had tumbled down to my lower floor room, suitcases knocking into tight hallway walls, until I opened the door and fell headlong into the soft mattress. It felt good to stretch out, all six feet four inches, and I was soon fast asleep. I woke up for a brief time in the dead of night, switching on the bedside lamp and reading a bit further into a weathered paperback copy of the *Autobiography of William Butler Yeats*. While lying there I noticed two portraits on opposite walls: one of John Kennedy and one of the Pope in Rome. It was the seated figure of John XXIII. Both men were smiling, sacred in the eyes of God. It was reassuring to lie there knowing that such charity was looking down on me.

Once awake, I showered and headed upstairs to the reception area. I had a few prepared questions in mind but instead of stopping and chatting with the older matron at the desk, I walked outside onto the sidewalk. It was a cool day with passing white clouds and alternating sun and shadows. People were passing by as were cars and lorries out on the street. Still feeling a bit dreamy, I had this sensation of looking out onto a movie scene as if I were watching the action from a far distance. Everything seemed different: the clothes, people, storefronts and even the smells and language. So, this is Dublin, I thought. My attention then turned to a group of people standing directly across the way, their backs turned to me and their interests focused towards a playing field of some sort. I walked over to their location and sat down on a grassy bank a few feet away. There before me was a match in progress, men in white clothes scattered about with a pitcher and pegs in the ground and a batter holding a rectangular paddle. What is this, I wondered. It looks like baseball but isn't. It must be an Irish game of some sort. After a few minutes, I stood and walked further down the street, eyeballing older women pushing small grocery strollers and men in dark hats with newspapers tucked under their arms. On impulse, I stepped into a pub and strolled up to the bar counter. It was dark inside with wooden chairs and tables and low-lit hanging lamps. I looked at the selections, not recognizing many of the choices and ordered a familiar Heineken. It came in a pint glass, a good full size, golden and topped with a ring of foam. Soon I was sitting in a corner booth, looking out a window onto the street scenes, enjoying the taste and sensations of the Irish atmosphere.

Later in the day, I made my way out to University College Dublin by way of city buses. The kind matron in the hotel saw fit to help me find my destination. She was a gregarious person, witty and good-natured, and full of kindly advice. I told her I was in Dublin to begin a graduate program at the college next week. I would be studying Irish literature.

"Reading, is it," she said. "I have little time for the likes of that, ah, but the best of luck to you, young fella."

She exchanged some money for me and pulled out her Dublin maps and wrote down the bus stops and street names and transfer points that would lead me to suburban Belfield where the college was now located. I was heading to the housing office as recommended in my college guidelines. There I would find information on where one might live in this city once referred to by James Joyce as "dear dirty Dublin".

✢

The Catholic University of Ireland officially opened for business in 1854 under the rectorship of John Henry Newman, an ordained Oratonian priest who would later become a cardinal. The campus was then small, one building that in time became known as the Newman House, situated across the street from St. Stephen's Green. With student interest and growth, the Catholic university system eventually expanded into other Irish cities with each site referred to as University College. In Dublin, the classes and programs moved into Earlsfort Terrace and neighboring buildings in 1908, a short distance away from its original chambers. Here it stayed complete and ennobled until 1964, when University College Dublin (UCD) science students began taking their classes at Belfield, a halcyon environment on the edge of the city. In 1970, the Arts, Commerce and Law facilities opened at Belfield, welcoming a broad spectrum of both undergraduate and graduate candidates. I was one of those chosen many, traveling by bus out of Dublin proper on a shadowy day in August 1978, the commencement of classes soon before me, and the need for accommodations the task at hand.

✢

Walking into the housing office at UCD, I found two walls of posted listings and a large Dublin map divided into city sections. There were a few other students around and I soon fell into conversation with two of them. One was an American, Keith from Massachusetts, a newly arrived graduate student in Medieval Studies, and the other a Canadian fellow with curly reddish-brown hair known by the rather uncommon name of Cyril (I had seen or heard the name only once before in my short life; it belonged to my father back home in the States). In a matter of minutes, Keith and I decided to room together with Cyril opting for his own place. With help from the housing assistants, we scanned the Dublin map attempting to imagine such places as Rathmines, Ballsbridge, Black Pool, Ranelagh, Donnybrook, and Haroldscross. We settled on an upstairs (unseen yet checked and verified by the UCD housing authorities) two bedroom, available, furnished flat in Terenure, a little further out from the city center but well connected by tram lines to all points including Belfield. With a phone call, a notification of our UCD student status, and a written agreement on rent and utilities (signed right there in the housing office) we had procured a guaranteed place to live. It was simple and satisfying. We would move in the next morning with keys in hand.

We left the housing office together, a trinity, drawn to each other like moths to a flame, all three of us having traveled long distances alone and wary to arrive on campus at the same exact moment in time. It was a Tuesday with full days ahead of us before classes began the following Monday. Now settled and housed, Cyril mentioned an interest in traveling to the Aran Islands off the west coast of Ireland. We could learn a little history, do some sightseeing, relax and walk the beaches and cliffs. "What a great idea," we each pronounced. We agreed to rendezvous the next day at the central rail station downtown. The train would take us across the full width of the island to the Galway City docks.

✥

The boat trip to Aran was thirty miles of gently rocking sea motion. We had found a way across Galway Bay on a fishing trawler, a lone pilot and the three of us enjoying the warmish August day free of rain and winds. The closer we came to Aran, three islands sitting distant and isolated out in the Atlantic Ocean, the further we left the sights of Galway and the vanishing Connemara coastline behind. It was an idyllic trip and few words were spoken amongst us. The rolling of the boat and the freshness of the air was enough to leave us silent and contemplative.

We landed at the village of Kilronan on the island of Inishmore in the late afternoon. Hungry and sleepy, our first stop was a small inn where tea and bread were readily available and warm to the touch. We asked about local accommodations and were directed to a hostel down the road where young students often found rooms. It was there we headed next, travel bags and groceries in hand, the light beginning to wane in the sky, for a period of rest and reading before venturing out into the night to find a pub and dinner and our initial exploratory tastes of native black Irish stout.

✥

Inishmore turned out to be a land of remote and barren splendor. As we traversed the island over the next few days we found high descending cliffs, pounding surfs and rocky walls, cross-etched stone pillars, beehive huts, and miles and miles of limestone slabs covering fields as if once poured hot from a boiling cauldron and then left to cool and harden upon the earth. There was a rich tapestry of nature around us. At each bend in the road there might appear a sun-draped slope, or the sight of endless speckled gray-green water, or sudden rain squalls coming in from the Atlantic, or there growing amongst the steep crags, ferns and brambles of various shapes and colors. There were no trees, no turf to be dug in bogs, just a profusion of breezy cliff tops, stone pieces, breakers crashing onto hidden shoals, birds soaring overhead and the ever-changing sheens of light, pale gold and bright silvers and at times darkening black from passing clouds. The people who lived in these surroundings were a quiet sort. They went about their business with a nod and a smile and a quick good morning to you all, the women in their flannel skirts and paisley shawls and men in caps and sweaters. There was shopping to be done, seaweed to be collected at the low tides, sheep and goats to be tended and morning masses to attend. It seemed to be a routine yet enriching existence amidst signs and symbols of both ancient and contemporary life: thin roads with cars and painted shops alongside remnants of Celtic high crosses and monastic dwellings.

On our last full day on Aran, we traveled up the east coast of Inishmore to the prehistoric Iron Age fortress of Dun Aengus. Here we found a fortified enclosure backed up against high towering cliffs. It was said the Pre-Celtic "Fir Bolg" once lived here, Ireland's original mythical inhabitants. They surrounded themselves with terraces and triple concentric lines of stone wall defenses using the Atlantic sea cliffs as impregnable safeguards. There was only a single entrance to the interior, once heavily guarded and secured with quarried stones. Dun Aengus was a site of communal living, tribal in its origins, with a pagan population working nearby yet close enough to escape into the fortress when in danger. It stood alone, a monument to a long ago, thriving civilization.

As evening came on and we were preparing to leave Dun Aengus, I walked to the cliff edge and looked west across the Atlantic towards home. Off in the distance the reddening sun sat low in the sky partially blocked by horizontal clouds. It was a serene moment and I sensed a strengthening stirring within me. Maybe it was the spirits of the Fir Bolg drifting by, lending me a hand, bestowing upon me a gift of empowerment. They were speaking to me, whispering in hushed tones... "Welcome ... you have come a long way to stand on ancient ground ... take a moment and rest before going onward ... to destinations ... to aspirations yet unfulfilled."

## 22

## Meeting James Joyce

Living in Dublin was a step into the old world. The city seemed worn and tired. Around every corner and down the public lanes one would come across history in the shape of stoic monuments, government buildings, artifact museums, aged pubs, hidden canals and in the middle of it all, the River Liffey tumbling down from the neighboring Wicklow Mountains through the heart of the city and out into Dublin Bay. It was a metropolis of brick and colored doors and wrought iron gates and decrepit lots and tinker caravans and green-laced flowering parks and people flowing in all directions, on and off two-story buses into cafes and shops, parcels in hand, silently engaged in the daily business of life. The air in Dublin was often moist and breezy, and the sky full of moving clouds. Now and then the sun would peek through, a surprise guest, reflecting off the wet and shiny sidewalks. Though a bit tattered, I found the city to be a place of captivating energy. It rose each day to tea, scones, newspapers and the talk of the town. It was spirited and alive with arts, politics and religion, yet also duly reserved, a smaller town ambiance of walkers and talkers, mostly circumspect and humble.

My graduate program in Anglo-Irish Literature began on a pleasant September afternoon at the Belfield campus of University College Dublin. A reception had been arranged for new M.A. and Ph.D. students in a room on the second floor of the admissions building. Here I found white cloth-covered tables laden with drinks and assorted food items. The room itself was brightly lit, enclosed by surrounding windows looking out onto green leafy trees. It was an atmosphere both warm and welcoming, with faculty members and students mingling about engaged in introductions. Within minutes I had met a number of fellow classmates, most of whom like myself had journeyed to Ireland from U.S. locations, places like Philadelphia, Denver, Lowell, and St. Louis. I soon discovered others: a European student from Belgium and native-born Irish students from both the Republic and Northern Ireland. It was a mixture of accents and faces, brief moments of conversation and fact-finding, a lively and exciting interchange of names, backgrounds and current Dublin dwellings.

At one point in the reception all eyes were directed to the front of the room where faculty members had gathered along a wall. Up stood Professors Roger McHugh and Augustine Martin, the current and soon-to-be chairman of the graduate program, and, as I was later to learn, distinguished teachers and scholars. Professor Martin's voice was rich and melodious, that of a poet, ringing with Irish passion and lore, as if he were singing a song to all those gathered near and far. I was mesmerized listening to his opening remarks. He outlined what was to come: term classes, thesis requirements, reading lists and final examinations, important dates and guidelines and an array of academic expectations. His messages rang true; embrace the learning before you, think for yourself, and find passion in the written and spoken word. Professor Martin may well have been saying, "Listen to me now," like so many Irishmen in conversation before and after him. There was reverence in his voice, instilled within a warm and lively presence. He had my full attention. In the back of the room I stood, eyes agleam in admiration, looking out over my newly recognized classmates. I couldn't wait for classes to begin.

✢

By the end of November, I had adapted to the flow of both graduate courses and urban living within Dublin city. It was around this time that I relocated from my original lodgings in Terenure to a one-room bedsit at 77 Beechwood Avenue in the neighborhood of Ranelagh. I was now closer to the city center and popular Grafton Street. There were also classmates nearby, people who were once acquaintances now becoming companions. Together, we would travel to and from the university, share meals, and frequent cozy, warm, around-the-corner pubs in the evenings. The weather was getting colder and wetter, so I made the circuit of discount markets off a downtown street, picking up a pair of sturdy shoes and a used horsehide-leather jacket. Along with a scarf and umbrella, I felt more amply prepared for the damp, wintry weather blowing off the tumultuous Irish Sea. Each school day there was time for classes, studying, cooking, some letter writing and a brisk walk. Off I would go into the streets of Dublin, destinations mostly unknown, huddled in my jacket with the collar turned upward, side-stepping native Dubliners, loose dogs, and cars weaving in and out of backwards traffic. The idea was to inhale fresh air, to become transient and discover Dublin by foot, and in doing so find a soothing rhythm to my stride. With time to spare here and there, I would extend the walks down along the Grand Canal all the way to Ringsend and up the River Liffey quays to the city center and then to avenues leading back into the storefronts of Ranelagh. These experiences helped to clear my mind, to let my thoughts flow without structure or purpose. I would at times relapse into wavering memories of home and an accounting of past events. It was all good and at the end of each walk I felt renewed and better prepared for another round of concentrated reading and note-taking.

The second term of studies began in early January with three classes, one of which was a symposium course on James Joyce's novel *Ulysses*. Of all the various offerings on Irish prose, poetry, drama, Hiberno-English, and specific writers (Samuel Beckett, James Joyce, Sean O'Casey, John Synge and W.B. Yeats), this was the class I most anticipated. We had been advised to read Joyce's *Dubliners* and *A Portrait of the Artist as a Young Man* as part of a summer reading log prior to fall enrollment. I had done so and found his descriptions of Irish life both distinctive and creative. Joyce was a writer of great linguistic talent. This was poignantly evident in all his writings. And his characters, especially Stephen Dedalus in the *Portrait*, were notable in terms of dialogue, self-awareness and intuition. Though I had once before completed a read-through of *Ulysses*, the story had left me floundering in periodic confusion. Portions of the book seemed to be somewhere beyond clear comprehension. I knew of Leopold Bloom and his wife Molly and the appearances of Stephen and others within *Ulysses* but not the full extent of the novel's themes or genius. So a course dedicated to the reading of *Ulysses* (a book considered by some to be the greatest novel of all time) was welcomed. And Joyce himself was an alumnus of University College Dublin. A son of Catholic parents, well-educated in the classics, he was in his day a youthful and frequent wanderer of Dublin streets until a self-chosen literary exile in mainland Europe. At the time, I felt we might share a common thread, Joyce and I, something to do with church affairs, literature and university life. I was eager to find out.

✢

It came to pass for myself and others that the academic reading journey through *Ulysses* began to mirror our own escapades within Dublin. Instead of haphazard treks, we began to follow the imagination of Joyce via the footsteps of Leopold Bloom and Stephen Dedalus. It never seemed to be intentional, but off I might go alone or with friends on a fair Saturday morning, drawn to featured places in Joyce's picturesque Dublin. One day might be a trip to the Martello Tower near Dun Laoghaire and then a beach excursion to Sandymount Strand, and on another day a stroll along the Liffey to the National Library and St. Stephen's Green, and, on still another, an evening sojourn to the Brazen Head or Davy Byrnes' pub. Joyce was a connoisseur of ordinary people living compelling lives of daily enterprise. Leopold Bloom was one of these and *Ulysses* is a story of one single day in his life attending to such matters as eating lunch, visiting an art museum, placing a newspaper ad, stopping by a funeral, buying breakfast meats, having a drink in a pub and serving tea to his wife Molly in bed. Bloom depicted the everyman: bereaved father and isolated husband, practical entrepreneur and wandering Jew, alone and thoughtful and charitable, at moments feeling like a stranger in his own land. He was graced with insightful ruminations and troubled reminiscences and hopeful aspirations. Dublin was his home and the dingy lanes, food markets, bar counters, and public places, his chosen domains. Throughout

*Ulysses*, when crossing paths with Stephen (the intellectual and brooding young poet haunted by his mother's death), Bloom would stop and bid hello and make a welcoming gesture. Though simple in his wants and desires, Bloom maintained a heightened sensibility. He was aware and empathic. Joyce provided him the sights, sounds, smells, colors and tastes of Dublin. He, Stephen and the other passing Dubliners in *Ulysses* came to represent the gentility, community, wit and imagination, and at times the vulgarity and seedy exterior, of their epoch. Yet they were sympathetic and human in all their discourses, a trademark of Joyce's characters.

There were brief occasions during this time of *Ulysses* immersion that I would catch a glimpse of Bloom or Stephen passing by on the Dublin streets. And Joyce himself was in the crowd, over yonder in the corner at the rounded table neatly dressed in hat and tie, sipping white wine and watching what he called the "hundred-headed rabble of the cathedral close". Oh, I knew this couldn't be true. It was well past Joyce's time and those other two were just fictional individuals from a book. Yet, look, there's a distracted Leopold crossing the street; over there, the artist hero Dedalus keeping to the shadows; and just now coming in the door, the villainous Blazes Boylan. At the sound of a cane striking the pavement, I would turn and see Joyce disappearing around a corner, the small man that he was, irascible and destined for greatness. Dublin was and remains today a city full of characters, alive and well through the ages.

✣

A certain night returns to me again and again in retrospect. A classmate and I had walked from Ranelagh down past Earlsford Terrace to the Newman House across the way from St. Stephen's Green. Upon entering we were ushered into a room where a group of people sat quietly reposed, sitting in chairs, books in hand, awaiting the commencement of an event. It was the James Joyce Institute of Ireland and on that evening there was to be a reading. Without much ado, the books were opened and a page announced. Up rang the sounds of Joyce's voices. Someone and then another were reading from the novel *Finnegans Wake*, Joyce's last literary achievement. Sitting quietly and listening with rapt attention, I heard the night music, the poetic nuances, the language of dreams, and further away the constant stirring of water. Somewhere beyond that sanctuary, out past the Green, down below Grafton Street and beyond, I felt the

River Liffey, Anna Livia Plurabelle, flowing past.

*"A way a lone a last a loved a long the*
$\qquad\qquad\qquad\qquad\qquad\qquad$*Riverrun."*

# 23

## Crossroads

The Irish Studies program came to an end on a cloudy September 1st in 1979. On that day, while feeling bitten by both a sense of accomplishment and finality, I made my way to the graduate program office at University College Dublin and officially submitted the final copy of my thesis. It was a culminating project, a typed and thoroughly considered paper representing all I had learnt and knew about Liam O'Flaherty. I had spent the summer researching and writing the thesis, a typical day consisting of a trip downtown to the National Library to review literary criticism and to read deeper into Mr. O'Flaherty's short stories and novels. Then came the long hours of writing and revising. It became an intensive analysis of a complete body of literature, all that O'Flaherty had written and placed on the Aran Islands as a setting for his varied literary themes and encounters. Putting the thesis in the hands of the graduate office accompanied by my closing signature was like turning a page, ending one chapter and beginning another. I was to leave Ireland the next morning, destination west by northwest. The Irish experience was coming to a close, engaging and bountiful though it was, with friends and classmates also scattering away. I was thankful for all that had transpired: the learning, the companionship and the personal growth. Ireland would remain a favorite venture point for years to come, a second home for heart and mind, as lush and emerald as a glorious day amongst the greenish seascapes of Puget Sound.

I landed by plane in Seattle anticipating a warm welcome. Someone with whom I had grown closer would be awaiting my arrival. Katherine had previously spent two months in Ireland during my academic tenure, visiting and working in Dublin. We had lived together in a small studio bedsit, modest and discreet, with a single enclosed communal bathroom at the top of the stairs, sink, toilet and tub with a plastic bucket at hand for impromptu showers. During her time in Dublin, Katherine was employed as a waitress and quickly came to embrace the endearing Irish people as well as my graduate school compatriots. We had also traveled to the south and west of Ireland enjoying picturesque moments in Doolin, Dingle, and Tralee. There was already much between us including growing notions of kinship and love. Upon meeting again in the airport, we hugged, smiled and walked out to the car, suitcases in tow and hands entwined. These were to be the first steps of a continuous life relationship leading in due time to marriage and children.

Initially, I couldn't find my bearings at home. I felt out of place, disoriented and listless, like a ship adrift on a moonless night. Something had happened to me in Ireland, a complete separation from all that I had once known. Distance and experience had anchored me elsewhere and coming back to live with my parents and start anew left me with feelings of trepidation. As it happened however, it was a brief stay in Tacoma, a few days or so, before Katherine and I departed on a road trip circumnavigating several western states. It was now her fourth year of medical school and time to interview for potential residencies. I was to be her traveling companion, her present and potential future partner in the likelihood of all things possible. It took two weeks, journeying from state to state, eyes glued on passing American landscapes, before I once again began to feel a little more at ease with the world.

I was now in transition, at a crossroads, between years of academic advancement and an immediate need to become self-sufficient and financially secure. Staying with my parents was necessary at first but uncomfortable. They were kind and accommodating, yet I was too old, too self-aware, and too proud to stay for long. At a low moment, fortune found its way to my doorstep (as it is known to do). Having taken a job at Fick Foundry, I suffered a broken hand on the first evening graveyard shift. Since I had worked there before during college, I was entitled to state-funded Labor and Industries Workman's Compensation. Within two weeks, I received my first check (back hours included) enabling me to rent a cheap apartment on Broadway Avenue overlooking the same industrial area where the large orange square doors of Fick could be clearly seen in the distance. I would often sit on my front porch deck at night, the immense array of lights and the sounds of the Tacoma tideflats shimmering below me, and thank God for unexpected pleasures. I had cash in the pocket, a one-bedroom, rickety, view apartment, a girlfriend of admirable character, and moments of enduring faith. I would find my way through this passage. Patience and perseverance were called for. I just needed to keep my eyes and ears open for all beneficial opportunities.

The first action I took was to schedule an appointment with the CETA office in downtown Tacoma. This was a government-sponsored career employment service. Though not entirely honest, I talked my way into a temporary job placement at Gray Middle School where I would be assisting students in a Reading Lab. The idea greatly appealed to me. The prospect of becoming a teacher was on my mind, circling in and out of contention as I pondered the future. Yet uncertainties held me back. Being a literature student was not the same as standing in a classroom delivering lesson plans and lectures. I recognized good teachers, masters of their craft, brilliant in knowledge and articulation. As yet, I did not see those traits conspiring within myself. So, an entry into a public school setting might provide me with experiences of unforeseen value.

This proved to be true. I spent the next three months sitting with seventh-grade students in both a classroom and tutoring space. We would read to each other, sounding out words, practicing pronunciations, slowly working our way through complete sentences and paragraphs. A structured curriculum was provided, a so-called reading map to follow enjoining instructional strategies, assignments and outcomes. I found the process enjoyable and eye-opening. For some students, it was a difficult struggle to read, to find an easy passage through sounds and words. Yet they persisted, intent on making progress, on keeping up with same-age classmates. I was humbled by their personal efforts. I was also impressed by the school, by the quality of the teachers and staff, and by the encouragement and support so freely proffered within the building. I came to know the school librarian (a person of sharp intellect) and the school social worker (a calm and considerate justice advocate). Over time, lunch hour conversations with both of these individuals enabled me to see beyond classroom teaching, to understand their own unique and important roles in education. In January, when the CETA contract came to an end, I was better informed about schools, having now sat on the other side of the desk. I was also intuitively inspired by all that I had experienced.

From there, the turning of days and nights carried me forward through the winter months until a defining moment over the Easter holiday weekend in April. I was by then working in my parents' accounting firm, learning the business in simple steps, and also traveling a bit here and there with my father to conduct financial audits. It was the first time I had ever worked with my parents: my father, the suit-adorned C.P.A. known as "Mr. G" and my mother, the efficient and ever pleasant bookkeeper. It was a rewarding experience allowing for both positive parental interactions and much-needed employment as I slowly settled back home in the Northwest. My relationship with Katherine was likewise blossoming during this time. There were trips to Seattle to meet and date, mostly evening outings at restaurants and movie houses, and on Sundays, dinner with her family or mine, a chance to learn more about each other in the context of home settings, family members and neighborhood friends. We were quickly building a bridge from one to the other, anchoring support beams from heart to heart, and finding strong and enduring connections.

It all came to a head on Easter Sunday as we sat outside her family home in Kent. We had gone out to the front porch to talk, escaping a sudden windy downpour by jumping into her blue Volkswagen Beetle parked out front. It was dark so we turned on the engine for heat and comfort, sitting close, just inches apart in the bucket seats, our faces aglow in the dim panel lights. Something had brought us to this moment in time: the religious weekend symbolized by renewed life and resurrection, the just completed dinner with her family and visiting relatives (including an uncle ordained as a Methodist minister), and the fact that Katherine would very soon be completing medical school and leaving Washington State. We were at a decision-making moment; to be or not to be, to join together or drift apart separately. We looked into each other's eyes, spoke a few opening sentences, exchanged mutual affirmations, then conceptualized the future flashing before us and decided to get married. Once back inside the house, we announced our plans and asked her uncle if he might conduct the ceremony in June. He agreed amidst applause and surprised faces. Our future was set; no longer at an undefined crossroads, we would journey forth together, for better or for worse, in sickness and in health, until death might split us asunder.

In due course after a medical school graduation and a Brown's Point sunny day wedding, Syracuse, New York became our new home. This too involved a road trip: a journey east on Interstate 90 through the fallen ash of Mount St. Helens with side trips to Yellowstone, the Black Hills, homes of relatives in South Dakota, Minnesota and Wisconsin, then Sault St. Marie, Canada, and across the St Lawrence Seaway into north central New York. We would stake our claim near the Erie Canal, determined to create a life partnership of reliance and distinction.

# 24

## Upstate

We arrived in Syracuse, New York as a recently married couple amidst a fading evening sunset. Having traveled south for most of the day, it felt like we were descending into the city from a higher elevation, the hill country to the north, passing by small towns and farms and then suburban villages perched alongside the interstate. Kingston had been our starting point, up in the Thousand Islands' region where we had stayed a few days enjoying forest scenes and water vistas. Lake Ontario was nearby, the easternmost of the Great Lakes, serving as a watery boundary between the state of New York and the Ontario region of Canada. This was new country for us, sights unseen, plentiful in natural spaces and historic folklore. I remember wondering while gazing out the car window where the French fur traders might be and the legendary Indians of the League of Five Nations. In the preceding days the land had spoken to us through the sounds of whispering trees and flowing rivers. And now Oneida Lake was nearby and beyond that the Adirondack Mountains to the east. All this and more we knew or had seen as urban Syracuse came into view, our future home and the end of a long cross-country trek.

We missed the downtown exit having not paid close enough attention to map-aided directions. This brought us to the next off ramp, south of the city center, into a neighborhood of old and forbidding brick structures and trashy sidewalks. I was feeling disconcerted as darkness quickly fell upon us. My safety alarms were on red alert inside my mind: Watch out! Be aware! Steady! You must find your way out of here to your designated location! Next to me, Katherine sat calm and collected, advising me to relax and stay cool. With patience in hand, she guided us back into the main streets of downtown and a hotel's front doors. Soon we were enclosed in our room, tired and travel weary, but snug as bugs in a soothing bed. In the morning, we would go forth, intent on finding our way to both the hospital and university campuses.

It turned out that both of these enterprises were adjacent to each other on a hillside overlooking the city business area. The Upstate Medical Center where Katherine would soon begin a residency in Pathology was a bit closer to the city, parking lots below and hospital and research buildings climbing higher onto the steep hill. Syracuse University, where I had been accepted as a graduate student in Library Science (my next educational endeavor), was further back, behind and across a street from the medical structures, also situated on a rounded slope, yet interlaced with sweeping lawns and ornate buildings. We spent the first day checking in, Katherine and then myself. We picked up orientation materials and schedules and met with administrative personnel. The residency program had also secured for us a month-long rental contract in a nearby apartment. So we had a temporary place to live and a plan of action. Katherine would begin her much anticipated residency on July 1st and I would scour the employment want ads hoping to find a part-time job to supplement my upcoming graduate studies.

It didn't take long to land an opportunity. Walden Books was opening a new store on the main street in downtown Syracuse and I was hired as a thirty-hour per week Assistant Manager. Though never having worked in a bookstore before, I definitely knew something about literature and other humanities and social science topics. It turned out my educational successes served me well in this circumstance, as it did for the person hired as manager. His name was Art, a recent college graduate himself, full of humor, wit and knowledge, and a native resident of the area. In time, he would become a good friend and companion to the both of us, loyal and true blue, a centerpiece of our lives in Syracuse. His nearby family, parents and sister also welcomed us into their circle with outstretched arms. We were readily enfolded in their care and consideration.

The wonders of upstate New York soon revealed themselves to us in dynamic fashion. As the hot, humid summer (alive with the shrill sounds of cicadas) passed into the zenith of autumn, we were greeted by dazzling leaf colors. Nothing we had ever seen before compared with the bright foliage within our neighborhood. We had moved by this time into the Eastwood district of Syracuse, situated up and over a hill and featuring a meandering park and sidewalks bordering tree-lined avenues. Directly out front and to the right of our screen-porched apartment stood two large Sugar Maple trees ablaze with color and movement. On a sunny day, the light reflected off the orange, yellow and red leaves creating its own abstract illusions. This light would pierce our windows, dancing off the walls, holding me spellbound as I sat in a study room momentarily turned away from books and notes. It was an eye-pleasing clamor of hues and shapes. So much so that we took repeated occasions to go in search of even greater color abundance, traveling out beyond Syracuse southwest to the Finger Lakes and northeast to what would become a favorite destination, the Sylvan Beach community on Oneida Lake.

It was also during these autumn months that I came to a realization that would change my life path forever. As my first semester enrollment in Library Science progressed, I became increasingly dissatisfied with the content and eventual career direction of the classes. The program felt too technical, too esoteric, and too far removed from the complex life in books I greatly admired. Each school day I would walk into the School of Education building, Huntington Hall, feeling downcast. I began to sense I was in the wrong major - that I had made a mistake. It was a troubling thought which slowly chipped away at my confidence. If it was not to be teaching, nor Library Science, then what? I was at a loss. However, I continued with the fall courses, striving to earn credits and worthy grades. Through the doors of Huntington Hall I would go, persistently aware of my personal dilemma, past the offices of other graduate programs, up the stairs and into waiting classrooms. And then one day, I stopped and sat down on a bench across from the doors of the Counseling & Guidance program. I had noticed this office before and had been intrigued by the students coming and going through its glass-paned entrance. Its two interconnecting ideals seemed to hold importance for me. Especially "Guidance", a word I looked at closely, etched there beside the door. I felt its significance, its mystique associated with a guiding light, or a guide leading the way through difficult passages. It held my attention, caught my interest, and ever so gently began to stimulate my soul. Its allure seemed to hold a double meaning; it sang to me of my own need for guidance at that particular moment in time and it also offered a possible change of direction, a new curriculum and degree, something more personal and empathic. So I stood up, walked across the hallway, opened the door and stepped inside. And there standing at the reception counter was a small balding man, a smile spread far and wide across his face, with a hand stretched forward ready to embrace my own. "Welcome," he said, "you have come to the right place."

This brilliant yet unassuming person was Dr. Alan Goldberg, an esteemed professor in the Counseling & Guidance Department. He invited me into his office for a chat where we remained for an hour or more conversing on various subjects including my own educational history and aspirations and the components of the guidance degree. At one point he informed me that English majors were often some of their best graduate students. It had much to do with their writing and communication skills as well as a keen awareness of personality and character. Near the end of our talk, he stated that I would be a good candidate for the counseling Master's program. He was impressed by my background and spoken interests. And since I had already been accepted into the Syracuse University Graduate School, I could change over at the semester into a new major if so desired. "Take some time to think about it," he suggested, "a week or more and come back and see me." In the meantime, he would review my graduate application file which contained written essays and letters of recommendation.

And so I did, walking to and from work and the university, stopping by the library a time or two to scan counseling-related books, and gradually adding up my past learning experiences to see if all roads might lead to a guidance vocation. In time, I came to the following conclusion: literature had been a first love, English a consummative major in college, and writing often a source of deep contentment. In retrospect, it was literature that led me to an analysis of language and language to writing and writing to reflection (of self and others) and now possibly reflection to a tenure in counseling. For me there had always been something important about language, written or spoken, about searching with words for a better understanding of life, and about breaking through silence and coming forth with a voice all one's own. It all seemed somehow tied to counseling, to personal acknowledgement and exploration. I was soon convinced changing my major was the right decision.

Syracuse became a home away from home for the next three years. The interweaving seasons brought abundant snowfalls and short-lived spring awakenings and the dog days of August and then once again the magical mysteries of fall. Within the discoveries of place, we also ventured through an infant marriage, itself a process of discovery, seeking, finding and enhancing each other in newness and fondness amidst the passing of time and circumstances. Each of us was experiencing change, far away from the well-versed notions of family, walking alongside each other, engaged in active learning and mutual growth. We had found an even stride, a spot to land and spread our wings, a place to nest and settle. Much was happening to us and between us and within us: cooperation, depth of feeling, integration, and trust. We looked into each other's eyes and saw love and support; we looked into the mirror and saw hope and destiny, the emerging lives of a physician and a counselor. It felt right and good, the beginnings of something greater than itself.

Our rituals in Syracuse, however, came to an unforeseen ending. Tragedy struck in Washington State. We left the Upstate region sooner than expected, a full year in advance, to return and lend a helping hand. Family was calling and we were needed and we needed them. One mother was suddenly gone and the other in the deadly grips of cancer. Life had proved to be tenuous; two living flames once so bright and nurturing now faded into darkness. We were all experiencing sorrow, grief and hardship. First though came a graduation (a Master's in counseling) and an early end to a medical residency (to be resumed in Seattle). In sadness we packed our bags and loaded our possessions into a truck. This time our travels would take us west, back towards the Cascade Mountains and Puget Sound. There we would pick up the broken pieces, embrace and endure, and move forward into a brittle future.

# 25

## Rehabilitation Road

I sat down across from Beverly hoping she might lift her head a bit and look me squarely in the eyes. We were sitting in her small ground-level apartment, the furniture old and shabby, the air smelling of cigarettes and stale food. There was a wooden coffee table between us, a few magazines on top and an ashtray filled to the edges with brown filter butts. I waited a moment in silence, allowing her time to compose herself, to find the words that might best describe her present situation.

In days previous, I had called Beverly by phone introducing myself as her newly-appointed Vocational Rehabilitation Counselor. I had been contracted through the State of Washington to assist her in a rehab process. As an injured person subsisting on workmen's compensation and other social service amenities, Beverly was totally dependent on state aid. She had not been employed for months, had not looked for nor applied for any jobs in recent times, and, as I was soon to learn, could barely move about her apartment due to persistent health issues. She was also a chain smoker, habitual daytime TV viewer, someone alone and without reachable family, and a soft-spoken, modest individual.

Beverly shifted in her chair and looked up at me with an expression full of pain and uneasiness. I noticed the shiny teardrops in her eyes and behind them hints of fear. Her first words came out hesitantly, one word tumbling over the other. "Would you like a cup of coffee?" she offered. I declined and thanked her for her kindness. Leaning forward, holding her eyes with mine, I stated that I was there to assist her, to act on her behalf as a counselor and advocate, with the goal of helping her find her way back to an independent and productive lifestyle. She nodded and said she understood. "Will my checks keep coming?" she asked, the fear in her face suddenly more pronounced. "Of course," I responded, "as long as you follow all state-directed requests and guidelines."

"Oh," she softly said under her breath.

"Don't worry Beverly, I will explain everything to you. This will all become much clearer in the days ahead."

✢

Beverly had spent most of her adult years working in restaurant kitchens as a cook. This included fry shops, diners, roadside truck stops and even a late-night tavern or two. Over the years she had suffered burns, scrapes, cuts, punctures and broken toes - all hazards of the occupation. Like many of the other clients on my caseload, her life had been one of toil and labor, long hours of demanding physical work, day after day, one eight-hour shift after another often with overtime, bending, twisting, lifting, endlessly standing on sore and tired feet until a slip and backwards fall resulting, in her case, in an injured lower back. Then a physician evaluation, a dose of medication and an attempted back-to-work period with ever increasing pain, the injury limiting physical movement and endurance. Soon would come the inability to make it through a work shift, a temporary or permanent end to employment and a state-filed labor and industries claim. At some point, sooner (hopefully) rather than later, a counselor would intervene, making a phone call, setting up a home appointment, and initiating a process of recovery and return-to-employment job stability. This was the format, all good intentions invoked, each counselor trained and prepared professionally, each counselor dedicated to positive outcomes, and each counselor a firm believer in the principles of rehabilitation.

☩

There were many work days, with street maps spread on the car seat beside me, driving to and from appointments at residences sometimes dingy and disconcerting, at times down back alleys and dirt roads, into trailer courts and housing developments, eagerly looking for addresses on ramshackle apartment complexes, that I would pull the car over, stop, and ponder for a few minutes the nature of rehabilitation, the current task at hand. Thoughts would appear, temporarily present in my mind like leaves drifting by on the wind. Rehabilitate! Meaning to restore? Or to correct? Maybe to change directions? Or to bring back? Or recover? Or reform? Or possibly even to redeem. Like in the church, a resurrection of sorts. It might be all these things together, happening in tandem, each a spoke in a turning wheel. The word rehabilitation seemed to carry great significance. I looked and sensed a long road stretching out ahead, miles and miles of signposts serving as clues along the way, the client learning and progressing, obtaining new skills, until a release at the end, a new identity forged by intuition and determination. I also realized that I was a part of this process, a person present in the room, administering guidance. It felt invigorating, the whole affair, difficult at times yet a blessing, having been given the opportunity to lend support as a counselor, aiding and assisting in the rehabilitative course. These thoughts and more would linger and prevail as I sat alongside various side streets, enabling me to then go forward, placing the car in gear and turning out onto the road towards the next scheduled appointment.

☩

As a Vocational Rehabilitation Counselor, I came to experience humanity in many diverse shapes and hues. No one seemed immune from periodic hardships, whether it be in the workplace, home front or surrounding community. Each client had a story or two to tell, some full of promise but others tales of trauma involving self, family, friends or neighbors, the whole mess of mankind and womankind entangled in daily living. Yet, beneath the injuries, struggles, and difficult personal histories, there were episodes of remarkable courage and perseverance. I would ask my clients to engage in challenging experiences, to take necessary steps towards recovery, and they mostly responded with positive actions. A little faith and support went a long way. I believed in them and asked that they believe in themselves. It was an equal partnership, fair and honest. There were medical summary office visits with physicians and physical therapists, interviews with employers past and present (some jobs remaining on hold, new jobs possibly on the horizon), and trips to technical schools to discuss retraining and for some, GED/high school diploma completion. There were also important conversations about relationships, goals, addictions, finances, and dependent children. Each visit revealed something tangible, a word or statement or insight newly spoken and acknowledged like a door opening ever wider allowing in more light and personal understanding. Each client was looking for answers, soul searching, attempting to put back together pieces of a disassembled life. Rehabilitation became a pathway, a means to an end, the force that might guide them to health and prosperity.

✢

Beverly remained in a state of suspended illness. She didn't get better but never progressively worse. Time went by, a year then two, and she saw less and less of the world outside her apartment door. The consistent pain and troubling fears held her in check. I seemed to be one of few visitors, along with kind neighbors and distant relatives, who came her way. We had taken all the steps to achieve rehabilitation, Beverly and I, and we had come up empty. She stayed in contact with doctors and health practitioners, but did not return to work. The state checks kept coming, enough to provide rent and food and a little extra for conveniences, the ashtray on the coffee table endlessly full of stubbed-out cigarettes. I always thought of Beverly as kind and vulnerable, doing what she could with what she had. Eventually, she was transferred to a different counselor. I remember walking away from her apartment for the last time, feeling disappointed, having just said good-bye and good luck. I had wanted the best for her. We had both aspired to worthy outcomes. But it hadn't happened. Not yet, at least. Driving away, back on the Rehabilitation Road, eyes sullen but looking ahead, I also knew there was cause for hope, always cause for hope, no matter the circumstances.

✢

In recent times, the concept of rehabilitation has taken on a new dimension. Instead of being present as a helping professional, I have participated in the rehab process as a supportive family member. There I witnessed the disheartening experiences of addiction, the fallout of years of drug and alcohol use, the family upheaval and renewals of faith. It has been a process where I have not sat in the familiar counselor's chair - facilitating, clarifying and responding - but in the therapeutic circle beside others, individuals known and unknown to me, hearing the stories, providing feedback, reading and listening to letters, and searching for truth and honesty. There has been a commendable structure to it all: the AA principles, the accountability and ownership guidelines, the fishbowl exercises, the mental health approaches, and the continuous dedication to living each day, one day at a time, in recovery and sobriety. Respectable people from all walks of life have shared and lent their voices, the addicts and their wives and husbands, children and parents, aunts and uncles, brothers and sisters, grandparents and friends. In all the testimonies and recounting of past events, I have never heard overarching anger or abandonment (though these emotions might have resided close beneath the surface). I have heard anguish, disbelief and sorrow. Yet, even in the most troubling moments, care and love were evident, a moment's touch away, binding each to each. Through it all, the group work, the phone calls, the weekend visits, has come restored hope and pride. Together, we have all been reaching for a brighter future.

## 26

## Departures and Awakenings

It all came around to this: people leaving and others arriving. It made sense, being the natural order of things. Yet in each instance there was a certain unpreparedness, a surprise element, as if after a quick turn of the head the world had taken on a new shape. It was a time of saying good-bye and bidding hello; a period, four years in the making, of grief, joy, sorrow and celebration. It was life and death in front of us, full force, ready or not, requiring a response.

✢

The first to depart was Katherine's mother, Janet Seiler. One evening, alone and driving home south on Interstate 5, she likely fell asleep at the wheel, drifting off onto the shoulder of the road where an abandoned car waited in the shadows. An impact ensued and Janet died instantly. There were no good-byes, no time to reminisce or recollect, to add and subtract all that had taken place over forty-nine years of living. It was a sudden leave-taking, a death that came too soon and unexpectedly for such a kind and loving daughter, mother, sister and wife. In her wake, she left behind stunned and mourning relatives and friends, each of them suffering in tearful silence, each of them bravely holding on to whatever remained, seeking solace and comfort, each of them attempting to envision a world without Janet's radiant presence.

I first met Janet at the Seiler home in the Cambridge neighborhood of Kent. I was there as a Sunday dinner guest, sitting alongside the oldest child of the household, Katherine, a new-found companion. I immediately felt drawn to Janet, how could I not, as she greeted me with a warm smile and bright, glittering eyes. At the time she was wearing fanciful glasses, wing-like, and her hair was cut short with twirls. Janet seemed young, at least younger than many of the other mothers I had encountered, and there was a freshness in her nature. She would venture to and from the kitchen, bringing food to the table, a lilting laugh in her voice, taking care of all matters domestic and parental. I knew then that Janet would be an advocate, a considerate and sweet person, someone I could chat with as the Seiler family became ever more familiar.

This proved to be true. Over the two years leading up to an eventual June wedding with Katherine, Janet remained a loyal ally. Busy as a bee in most of her own affairs from mothering to shopping to cooking to sewing to orchestrating time-consuming ice skating practices and competitions for the two youngest daughters, Janet always found a moment to share an inviting smile and word with me. We would come and go, Katherine immersed in the last two years of medical school, often away at assigned rotations in hospital settings, and I traveling to Ireland for a year of graduate school, at first present, then gone, then reappearing, a person once again seated at the Sunday evening dinner table. It didn't seem to matter to Janet. Upon seeing one another after periods of absence, her welcoming disposition would shine steadfast and benevolent. I could feel her humility, came to appreciate her many notable talents, and always felt accepted in her home. (Not so with the father of the family, at first a distant and aloof man, unwilling to engage me in conversation, hidden in his own thoughts, a bright Boeing physicist encumbered by work and golf. Only later in future time would we find a respectful shared existence.)

I remember one night in particular sitting in the lobby of the Spaghetti Factory restaurant, awaiting a table, the evening of a Seiler family celebration, a birthday or anniversary, the father on the other side of the room still not speaking to me directly, when Janet came over, sat next to me placing a hand on my knee and whispered in the most gentle and soothing voice, "You are perfect for Katherine." It was all the approval I needed. She had sensed my discomfort and offered me reassurance. Go forward, she seemed to be saying, don't worry about others, take Katherine's hand, I see the love between you, the moment is now for the two of you to take action. And so we did. A wedding was planned and carried out, a mirthful occasion of sunshine, vows, congratulations and farewells. A few days later, we packed our bags amidst well wishes and headed to upstate New York. It was the beginning of our marriage years, away from home, chosen, yet far removed from familiar ties.

Time went by. There were visits back to Washington State for Christmas and special occasions. Letters were written and phone calls were made. A reaching-out took place, a way of sending our love thousands of miles across the U.S. continent. Then three years into our Syracuse sojourn came the early morning phone call and Katherine's anguished cries; Janet was no longer with us, gone the way of all saintly creatures, into God's abundant grace.

More than anything else, Janet's face lingers within memory ... the simple happiness in her glance, the telltale brightness within her voice, and the enduring kindness in her eyes. "Thank you," I say, whispering softly, "thank you for all that you were and still are."

✤

The first to awaken was Kevin Galagan. He was born on an early morning in late August before the sun came up, the stars above glowing bright and expansive in the sky. He was our first child, christened after St. Kevin of Glendalough, a peace-loving priest and founder of a monastic settlement and pilgrimage site in Ireland. We had visited there once, during our time living in Dublin - Katherine, I and two friends from Belgium, walking through the lush steep-sided glen, down through the Valley of the Two Lakes, standing among Celtic crosses, ancient churches, beehive huts, and an immense round tower. Our friends had made an announcement that day: they were soon to be parents. We celebrated with a picnic lunch, sitting together sharing bread and cheese, the landscape surrounding us alive with carved stones, glistening water and dark ascending trees. It was a special occasion in a holy place; St. Kevin the gentle one looking over us as we talked of birth and family.

Katherine's pregnancy was stable and well monitored. There were ongoing medical appointments, trips to maternity stores, fun-filled baby showers and a gradual transformation of a second bedroom into a nursery. At the time, we were renting a small bungalow house near Green Lake in Seattle. All through the pregnancy, we often strolled the path around the lake, talking and preparing ourselves for the changes ahead. Anticipation was the word of the moment and a pervading sense of excitement. All was going well. Janet was still in our thoughts as was the child yet to be born. We were together, united in our healing and hope.

The afternoon prior to the delivery we spent walking a pitch-and-putt golf course next to the lake as Katherine felt the first throes of labor. I would hit the longer shots while Katherine concentrated on mastering the greens. We took our time, one slow step after another, resting on the benches at each hole, letting others play ahead as we whiled away the time. From there we headed up to the Wallingford district for an Italian dinner and a movie at the Guild 45th Theater. The feature film was "Amadeus", a riveting presentation of the life and times of Wolfgang Amadeus Mozart, the genius-ridden childhood musical prodigy. As we sat in the darkness watching the stark confessions of Antonio Salieri being played out scene after scene, the music of Mozart began to envelope all present. It was a magnificent crescendo of notes: "The Marriage of Figaro", the "Requiem Mass in D minor", and Mozart himself directing "The Magic Flute". And there beside me folded inside Katherine was baby Kevin, soon to be a part of the known world, soaking up the symphonic and operatic vibrations. It was not many hours later that he came to us, all seven pounds eleven ounces, issuing forth with his own music: cries, gurgles and coos, the beginnings of his talking narrative, all of which have stayed with him to this day, now amply transformed into stylized lyrics and guitar riffs. Kevin either found the music or the music found him, but like Mozart and others he remains swayed throughout life by the sounds within his mind.

A loving first son he became, Kevin Joseph, a sensitive, bright boy with many insights and questions, happy and free and aware though wayward at times, struggling to find his rightful place in a confusing world, growing and learning, a philosophy major and voracious reader, a team-builder and hoopster, an older brother, himself eventually a caring father, and with time and age a songwriter and musician. He is here with us at this moment, in these words, nodding his head, tapping his foot, once so far away now closer by the day.

✢

The second to depart was Bernice Galagan. She was doing fine until a day when her balance was a bit off and the car just didn't want to drive in a straight line. She went in to see her doctor and was soon diagnosed with brain cancer. A surgery took place and a tumor was removed leaving her in a precarious state; greatly weakened by the operation, she slowly recovered at home under the affectionate care of her two daughters, Julia and Mary. But Bernice never really did find her way back to full strength. There were chemotherapy and radiation treatments, difficult but potentially life-saving interventions. However, a part of her had been compromised; it was all too much to bear, to overcome and to endure. She eventually settled into a nursing care facility, sharing time with family, friends and professional caregivers.

At the end, I received the phone call announcing her passing in sleep, a quiet death, peaceful and without struggle. It was late and the attendant nurse had not been able to reach my father (his phone would ring and ring without answer). So I drove down from Seattle to Tacoma near dawn, myself and a few other lonely night travelers on the road, to awaken him with the news. We sat in the bedroom, the one my parents had shared for what seemed an eternity, and momentarily cried together as he went about dressing and putting on his shoes. They had experienced a long life hand in hand, and this had been the final chapter. Bernice was no longer with us, she had passed along to a better place, one without pain and loss of dignity. It was a mixed blessing, the absence of someone irreplaceable, yet she was now free of the disease and sky bound, once again joining her own parents and sister who had journeyed before her into a heavenly kingdom. The rising sun greeted us on Easter Saturday. At Rosemont, we sat by her bed in silence looking down upon her tranquil face, my father and I both adrift in remembrance. I missed her then, deeply, and still do today, many years later, a long time since that weekend of resurrection.

In many ways, Bernice was an adventurous soul. She relocated as a young woman to Seattle, boarding a train in Minneapolis and stopping along the westward tracks to visit national parks and ride horses into the backcountry. I see her now standing atop a large rock, looking out over a valley, saddle pants sagging at the hips and black boots gleaming in the sunshine. In her eyes is a look of wonderment as if she was thinking, here is a good place to stop and look into the future. Maybe what she saw were the children yet to be born, six births between 1947 and 1959; four boys followed by two girls and like all children each with their own unique desires and needs. Did she know then that she would be a compassionate mother, always available, fair and supportive? Did she see the hardships to come and also the triumphs? Might the image of a rising sun have appeared to her, blazing above the distant mountains, foretelling the many years of life and her single day of death?

Bernice was sharp as a tack, becoming a bookkeeper by trade and a mystery reader by disposition. She loved her tea, a television game show or two, Sunday night Bonanza in the den with pans of popcorn, and a slow, contemplative cigarette after dinner. Just when you thought she was nowhere to be found, there she would be around the corner - ever present and watchful, never too far away, anchored in the home and family business. She often said to me in various ways, "Come here. What's new? How are you feeling? You are a good son. Go on. Find your wings. Don't forget to call home. Have fun. Eat lots of protein. Your family is important. Stand straight. I am so proud of you. With love now and forever."

✢

The last awakening was Sean Galagan. He was born on the third day of October, during a time of year when the leafy trees were bright in color and contrast. We were still living near Green Lake, the three of us, Kevin now in his twenty-sixth month and sprouting like a tree. The dimensions of pregnancy and birth this time around seemed a bit easier: the preparations and expectations and organizations more familiar and less surprising. Soon we would be a family of four. There were be an even number residing in the bungalow house. Two multiplied by two; two bedrooms, two children, two parents, and two cats. It all added up to a promising equation.

Again it was an early morning birth. For some reason the hospital setting seemed more vivid and bursting with energy this time than during the first delivery a few years before. It was the same place, Group Health on Capitol Hill in Seattle, yet there was a sparkle to the floors and walls making it all appear new and recently opened. I was in the birthing room, as once before, with the doctor and nurses and Katherine situated in the middle, the center of attention, working through a sequence of contractions. It didn't take long, hours compressing into minutes, and the baby was born.

"She is looking great," the doctor stated, lifting the little ball of flesh in his gloved hands.

"I mean, *he* is looking great," he quickly corrected, turning the baby around for a better view.

Katherine and I made double eye contacts during these announcements. Once for the baby girl and then a repeat for the baby boy. We smiled, then smiled again, happy all had gone well, mother and child in excellent health. Having not known the sex of the infant, the names hovered between us, Kara and Sean, with the latter lingering in our minds as he was cleaned and covered and placed in Katherine's arms. We now had two boys, brothers-to-be, and double the happiness and responsibilities.

There had been a few moments of excitement when Katherine first went into labor. We had arranged for our nanny, Jill, to be at the house watching Kevin while mom and dad hurried to the hospital. When the time arrived in the middle of the night to call her for a pick-up, her phone was silent. I quickly put on my shoes and coat and headed outside to the car letting Katherine know that I would go wake her up and be back in an hour.

"An hour?" I heard her shout. "No way. Make it 30 minutes at the most. I can't wait that long!"

I made the trip in a panic, driving like an Indy-500 driver and pounding on Jill's door while imploring her to hurry, hurry, hurry (she happened to live with my sister and their phone had been inadvertently unplugged). We reached the Green Lake bungalow, Jill and I, within the requested timeline, traveling in haste (stopping then running stoplights when the coast was clear). By the time we arrived at the hospital and Katherine was secure and under medical supervision, I felt a great weight of anxiety lift from my shoulders. It was then that I sat down in a lobby chair, closed my eyes and took a deep breath. Okay, I thought, we are off to an interesting start.

Sean was easy in mood and temperament from the onset. It was almost like he was giving us a break, as if he had witnessed the fast action beginning and decided to shift back a gear. All smiles and looking like a little bird, he came home in a day or so to meet his brother and stake his place in the household. Days went by into months and before long Sean was crawling and grabbing and speaking his first words, one of which was "mine", a sound he had repeatedly heard out of the mouth of his brother. The give and take had begun, the "I have, you have, we have" shared existence of growing inseparable siblings.

A loving second son he became, Sean Richard, curly blonde-haired and cute as the dickens, steady and fair-minded, a loyal friend and somewhat quiet lad, who early on loved staying up beyond bedtime and reading stories, deep and analytical like his maternal relatives, brilliant at math and science, a Biology major and public health advocate, a thrower of Frisbees, a bicyclist, a hiker, a jazz appreciator, and a younger brother. He is here with us today, close by, tending his garden, every now and then so far away, across the world yet never beyond reach.

# 27

# A Closing Hymn

In the concluding moments of the Mass the priest stood in front of the altar, arms raised and stretched outward, giving a final blessing as each person in the congregation made the sign of the cross, heads bowed, hands folded and most speaking within themselves, "In the name of the Father and of the Son and of the Holy Spirit, Amen." The last departing words, "Go in Peace, the Mass has ended" were followed by a stirring and shuffling amidst the pews as people exhaled, lifted their eyes and relaxed, feeling lighter before God's eternal presence. An announcement was made, "Please turn to page 109 in your red hymnals." In the back of the church, up above in the choir loft, the organ hit the first note and all eyes looked forward ready to begin the closing hymn. A raising of voices ensued, a singing out, an ode of praise and grace.

*Which brings me to the end of this narrative, this book, this recounting of memories long and not so long ago. Though the Mass has ended (and soon so too these chapters) and the closing hymn has concluded, the words and the songs still stay with me, invisible yet ever present. I carry them forward, etched in remembrance. When needed, I can travel back in time and find myself there again, the young boy at church, eyes gazing into the light, the music filling the air ...*

It was here, at this moment, time and time again, that I would feel the most devout. Whether I was standing up front on the communion rail steps, uplifted crucifix in hand and dressed in the black and white garments of an altar boy, or interspersed within the loyal faithful next to family or classmates, my breath would quicken and my mind would drift with the music - the words of glory and the veneration of all things holy and apostolic. Might it have been reverence I felt, a deepening mood of awe and respect for the church, its rituals and history, as if time itself had suddenly stopped, leaving me enraptured in place? There I would be immobile and content, not the person inching through life day after day encountering all sorts of puzzlements and schemes, but someone different, lost in empty thoughts, no needs or desires or pressing concerns, just the moment in itself, the voices, music and sanctity of the church.

*Then in a blink of an eye or the wave of a hand, the moment would be gone. The music would stop and the people would leave and time would move forward into a new day. I would walk outside the church, a few steps beyond holy ground, and begin to take up the tasks at hand. But something had happened, something I could feel then and still now as I write these words, something that has stayed with me through age and experience. Might it have been food for the soul, those words, music and spiritual mysteries? A recipe for self-awareness and understanding? Each episode providing a glimpse into the self, into the past and possibly even the future? And each episode leaving me with memories floating by here and there, visions vivid with colors, shapes and sounds. I remember now, places coming back through time and words ...*

St. Patrick's, a brownish stone structure sitting on top of a hill overlooking Old Tacoma, a place of Baptism, First Communion and Confirmation and where the funeral masses of my parents were solemnly performed. From there to the chapel at Bellarmine Prep, the Jesuits presiding over the services, some quietly traditional, others infused with guitars and the come-together folk music of the sixties. Then Seattle and Blessed Sacrament, representing my college years, a brick church I would visit on occasion, sitting in the back, private and away from others, contemplating all that was going well and all that wasn't. Later would come Ireland and its cathedrals and small neighborhood corner churches, the humble Irish people wrapped in dark sweaters and coats and lost in stoic prayer. Over time there were additional visits into European churches: Italy, Spain, France, Portugal, and other old-world settings and on occasion an opportune step into a Mass or benediction. Once settled and raising a family in Seattle and living on Capitol Hill, St. Joseph's became the center point: the school, the parishioners, and the church with its gilt-painted murals and gleaming stained-glass windows.

*At each stop, no matter the location, a sequence would transpire: the slow walk into the church and down an aisle, the immediate shadowing of quietude, the opening of the Mass, the readings, the taking of the Eucharist, the silent pleadings and enumerations, until the final blessing and peace-giving, each leading to the end, the apex of it all, the closing hymn, and the sendoff of resounding worshipful song.*

*It is the same in writing, in remembering, in silently sitting at a desk and calling forth memories in sentence form. There is a beginning and an end and a sequence in-between where one is lost in reverie and contemplation. Thoughts become notions and notions become images and images become meanings and meanings lead to insights and insights to words spoken or sung or written onto a page. Hence a story is made, a reflection of self and others. In the process there is stillness ...*

It was here I felt composed, at peace within myself, however briefly, and the most humane, all thoughts and actions gathered and held in place, silent with no movement, no purpose, just present and thankful.

*And so I bring this chapter, this book to an end. In the remembrance of peace and song, family and friends, here within this blue room, alone and in the cradle of the written word.*

Made in the USA
Lexington, KY
17 November 2017